Las hijas de Juan

A book in the series

Latin America Otherwise:

Languages, Empires, Nations

Series editors:

Walter D. Mignolo, *Duke University*

Irene Silverblatt, *Duke University*

Sonia Saldívar-Hull, *University of*

California, Los Angeles

Las hijas de Juan:

Daughters Betrayed

Josie Méndez-Negrete

Duke University Press

Durham and London 2006

Revised edition © 2006 Duke University Press
All rights reserved. First edition published 2002.
Printed in the United States of America on
acid-free paper ∞ Designed by Amy Ruth Buchanan
Typeset in Weiss by Keystone Typesetting, Inc.
Library of Congress Cataloging-in-Publication Data
appear on the last printed page of this book.

For Tía Hermelinda and all the
women who shaped and influenced
me to become who I am, I have written
this book.

Jorge, *mi querido esposo,* I thank you
for challenging and encouraging me to
write about my family's early years.

To my sons, Robert and Corky,
I appreciate the life lessons.

*A mi familia, que me apoyó y ayudó
a realizar mis sueños,* and especially for my
sisters, Mague and Felisa, but most of all
to Amá, who helped us reclaim ourselves,
I dedicate this book.

We must move beyond a celebration
of *la familia* to address questions of power
and patriarchy. . . . [Women's] legacies
of resistance reveal their resiliency,
determination, and strength.

Vicky Ruiz, *From Out of the Shadows:*
Mexican Women in Twentieth-Century America

Contents

About the Series

Latin America Otherwise: Languages, Empires, Nations is a critical series. It aims to explore the emergence and consequences of concepts used to define "Latin America" while at the same time exploring the broad interplay of political, economic, and cultural practices that have shaped Latin American worlds. Latin America, at the crossroads of competing imperial designs and local responses, has been construed as a geocultural and geopolitical entity since the nineteenth century. This series provides a starting point to redefine Latin America as a configuration of political, linguistic, cultural, and economic intersections that demands a continuous reappraisal of the role of the Americas in history, and of the ongoing process of globalization and the relocation of people and cultures that have characterized Latin America's experience. *Latin America Otherwise: Languages, Empires, Nations* is a forum that confronts established geocultural constructions, that rethinks area studies and disciplinary boundaries, that assesses convictions of the academy and of public policy, and that, correspondingly, demands that the practices through which we produce knowledge and understanding about and from Latin America be subject to rigorous and critical scrutiny.

In *Las hijas de Juan*, Josie Méndez-Negrete boldly shatters the silence surrounding a Chicana family tragedy. This intellectually astute *tour de force* builds on the tradition of Cherríe Moraga and Gloria Anzaldúa in its unflinching truth telling. These are the daughters who, in the face of the patriarchal imperative to put men first and condone their abuses, liberate themselves and dare to tell the tale. Méndez-Negrete weaves a complex tale of contemporary *mujeres de fuerza* and brings the fight for social justice to the previously protected fortress of the family.

Las hijas de Juan is a narrative of contemporary U.S. Latina life, anchored in the explicitly political tradition of *testimonio* exemplified by social activists such as Rigoberta Menchú, Elvia Alvardo, and Maria Teresa Tula. The author identifies the text as auto-ethnography, but at times it reads like a novel in the literary tradition of Ernesto Galarza's Chicano classic *Barrio Boy*. Méndez-Negrete never offers mere nostalgia; her paradisiacal life in Mexico, with its evocative tastes and aromas and strong network of women-centered households, is shattered by the reality of life under a violent, tyrannical patriarch. This is Latina *testimonio* at its most provocative.

Acknowledgments

Because of the support I received from my family, this book was possible. Over time, friends and colleagues have read and provided insight or comments on my work-in-progress.

For their invaluable gift of friendship and collegial support, I thank Dr. Candace West, Dr. Migdalia Reyes, Dr. Louis Mendoza, Sandra Cisneros, Dr. Norma Cantú, and Dr. Arturo Vega. I am indebted to Margarita Maestas-Flores for her invaluable editorial support on drafts of the book. To Gloria Ramírez for her guidance in helping me come to voice, I express special appreciation. Each and every one of you merits a *gracias* for your part in the process. Barbara Renaud González, for showing me the books within the book and for pushing me to tell the embedded story: *¡mil gracias!* Lilliana P. Saldaña and Carmen Guzmán-Martinez, I thank you both for your editorial support.

Finally, I offer a strong *abrazo* to my San José State University colleagues, Dr. Joan Merdinger and Professor Simon Dominguez—may he rest in peace—for their encouragement. Dean Sylvia Rodríguez Andrew, thanks for believing in me.

Author's Note

Because of the time elapsed since these events occurred, and, in some cases, the trauma of reliving these experiences, I have had to fill in some gaps. These *recuerdos* do not, however, distort the reality of what happened to my family and to me. Unearthing the bones I thought buried, I have had to reconstruct my recollections. This is a true story. It is no fabrication. Some names have been changed to protect the privacy of individuals who were in my life but not part of my family.

Prologue: *Sin padre*

I don't love my father. There is no reason to love him. Did my father love me? I don't think so. I was a girl. To him, I looked like anything or anyone but him. I was the child he didn't want. He wanted sons. He didn't want girls. He wanted sons to help him realize his dreams. We girls couldn't help him. We were a burden—another mouth to feed and another dependent to support.

As a young, handsome man in his twenties, he wanted to be the center of my mother's world. I, a *chingada muchacha*, took his place and his love. He found more than enough reasons not to like me.

But for my presence in the world, he would be an evil figment of my imagination. I write these words to understand myself as his progeny. I wish I could have loved him. Even though he was easy on the eyes, and a man born into my grandfather's legacy of respect, I lived in fear of him.

It's hard for me to find the love. He was a monster.

Still, there are memories, such as the way he danced. The way my mother loved him brings good thoughts about him. Are these reasons to love my father? I don't remember having been tucked into bed by him. I don't recall being praised for my ability to think or for being smart. My mother did all of that. At best, we played cards together. I don't remember how old I was, but he taught me to play gin rummy and casino. I was good with numbers, like him.

Although I worked in the fields with him, it wasn't love work—it was exploitation, a way of making more money as a family. It was a way for us to pay back for being born into his family.

Once we left Mexico, in the United States, we traveled like the gypsies of whom I had learned to be suspect—we seldom had the time to create a sense of community. Juan took my family and me from all we knew. He stripped us of the comfort of an extended family who loved and treasured us. Now captive, we lived inside the isolation of migration, ready for the abuse he might've planned to begin when he brought us here. Although our migration was geographical, we lived in the bounds of emotional turmoil. Here, we had to create a space for survival. Despite the displacement and our constant movement, we had no choice but to endure in our private home and in the farm work of which we became part.

A volatile man, he made us work for our daily bread. Juan wanted to show us what it was like to feed us. But it wasn't the fact that he had to support us that fed his ire; he was angry because we were girls. He needed boys to work with him.

Sunup to sundown, he worked. He worked hard.

For ten years he worked as a *bracero* in Texas. It was a good training ground for the abuses he would give later in life. He lived in chicken coops with a bunch of other men. The only time he had away from work was Saturday night. His U.S. dream had turned into a nightmare. Had it not been for his skills of relating to people and his willingness to live the city life, he would have stayed in the fields the rest of his life.

Father, I'm sorry you had such a hard life. Sorry I couldn't have made it better for you.

I have achieved the dream you could never reach, although it wasn't your intent. I forgive you for the pain and thank you for the gifts I have that you could never have.

Why did you have to make me fierce by abusing me? If only you had believed in me and loved me. If only I had been precious to you. If only you had recognized me as your daughter with all the respect and honor that having a child gave you.

I'm sorry that the land that rejected you tolerates me.

Thank you for bringing me to a place where I could become who I am, able to reach the dreams you should have had. I want you to know that your dreams live in me with the dancing, the poetry, and the artistic expression I inherited from you.

I love those things about you, although I despise the part of you that hurt me. Someday I hope to understand. One day I hope to forgive you as I have forgiven myself.

2

México lindo y querido

Dearest and beloved Mexico

Hijas de la tisnada

Never knew my father. The only memories I have of him are tied to abuse and violence.

Soy una hija de la chingada because I was born female.

For this accident of life, I am still trying to make redress.

As I continue to become whole, picking up the pieces like Humpty Dumpty to put myself together again, the frayed and mismatched edges leave gaps in my soul.

Exposed. These raw sites of pain never let me forget what I have experienced—the life I have had.

Keep me mindful of the hurt.

Serve as life guides. Don't let me forget.

Yagas and scars of life remind me not to hurt others because I have been hurt. That's how I try to live my life.

Hacha

Huele de noche, the sweet and spicy scent of the "smells-at-night" ivy, lingered like morning dew in the bright yellow and red colors of the sunrise. In that placid space, the madman's actions were out of place, capturing a vision of insanity. The only ones that seemed to notice were the caged birds whose song warned of doom.

He pulled her long, raven tresses toward the ground, as she hung on for dear life. She knelt next to a tree trunk, anchoring herself to its foundation. He cursed her for the delusional sins she had committed against him. Eyes bore the look of someone who would soon meet her demise.

As he paced up and down ranting and raving about this and that, he warned her not to move. For effect, he waved his ax in the air, slicing and dicing imaginary targets, threatening to chop off her head.

Feeling he had made his point, he stood erectly above her and lifted the ax to strike. But an invisible force stopped him.

He walked away, with no evidence of regret.

Faded into the landscape, leaving the woman he had promised to honor and to respect shaking with the knowledge that she had almost lost her life.

When he was finally out of her sight, she came undone.

Alejandrina, not yet my mother, cried tears I wouldn't see again until our family broke apart years later. Her sobs rocked the earth and made the winds blow—they screamed her pain.

I have lived thinking I had made up the story.

"Did he try to cut your head off?" in a scared, three-year-old voice I asked. I didn't expect a response, but one came.

Her face turned an ashen white, the blood draining from it. Her contorted grimace confirmed my memory, as she asked how I had learned about the incident.

"Who told you? ¡Nadie sabía! How did you find out?"

"No one told me. I saw the whole thing with my own eyes," I answered, hoping that the horror had been a figment of my imagination.

"You couldn't have. You weren't even born when that happened. I never told anyone."

With that story I finally learned why we came into each other's life. She came to care for me and to love me and I to love and to protect her.

Flor de nopal: The Courtship

We were supposed to live happily ever after, but el destino had other plans for us.

All who knew them swore that there was no love greater than the one my parents had for each other. Juan, my father, and Alejandrina, my mother, had been *novios* from across an arroyo that separated the properties of the Méndezes and Barrones. Their love flourished and grew with the waterfall that draped the limestone bridge that separated them. However, until they were married, all they could aspire to was conversation. Yet, like the creek, the *novios* also would have a path to follow.

Beyond the creek, under the watchful eye of Uncle Nacho, a fierce chaperone, her older brother and family patriarch, stood watch in the cactus garden that surrounded his property, keeping vigil over my father's intentions, acting like a sentry and a barrier all at the same time, protecting what was his. Uncle Nacho was like the *nopales*, with leaves and thorns that attracted and repelled those who wanted the harvest of his hard work. He hoped it would scare those who courted his younger sisters away. Uncle Nacho tended to his sisters and the *nopales* like the children he never had. He hoped his grouchiness and the cactus garden would protect his sisters' virtue. Everybody feared and respected him. Most young men would have stayed away.

For my mother the cactus garden was something altogether different. Its array of greens soon came to represent her feelings of hope for her growing love. Inspired by the eruption of yellow, red, and white flowers, which yielded delicious prickly pears, *tunas*, my parents' love grew more intense with each day that passed, blossoming with each of the petals of the cactus flowers that unfolded to yield their precious fruit.

My mother was known for her beauty. She had green eyes the color of the flesh that first peeks out when peeling an avocado and lips the color of a red prickly pear, perfectly shaped like an angel's heart. She was a Mexican Madonna like her grandmother Milani, who came from Italy. Her skin was the color of peach mother-of-pearl, her face crowned by soft waves of long, black hair. With a body that lined up men as *pretendientes*, she was shaped like a tango dancer draping the backdrop of the dance halls in Gardel's movies of yesteryear. With her voice froggy like Maria Felix's—the *Doña* of Mexican cinema—which they could detect even before she was in their midst, most people anxiously awaited mother's arrival. And, without fail, those who didn't know her often inquired if she sang. Many suitors in the region wanted her as their wife. She was the catch of the *rancho*. But it was my father with whom she fell in love.

Their *noviazgo* followed the script of a traditional text. My mother, restricted by conventions of chastity and virtue, kept her distance from my father. He, on the other hand, relentlessly wooed her with *cartas de amor*. Juan José, the macho child of Apolonio Méndez, who had been *presidente municipal*, was an excellent writer of love letters and a coveted catch by standards of wealth and prestige—*los Méndez estaban muy bién colocados*. His family had status in their community.

Mi madre venía de buena mata—she came from a family who was known and respected, from good people who were deeply rooted in that community. Her brothers and sisters were hardworking peasants whose communal lands had been in the family for generations. The Barrones were not poor; their hard-earned *cosechas*, livestock, and thriftiness kept them going from one season to the next.

Several harvests passed and the waters in the nearby arroyo ebbed and flowed. The end of their *plaso*—the waiting time imposed by Uncle Nacho when my father asked for her hand in marriage—finally came.

The day finally arrived. With a very formal wedding at Villa del Refugio Catholic Church, Alejandrina and Juan became *marido y mujer* in 1945.

Everything was expected to go well for them. But their marriage didn't start out that way. My mother had difficulty getting pregnant, casting doubts on her husband's virility. Some claimed it was then that he started abusing her. Others blamed her for her inability to conceive.

Women around town were heard talking about my parents' difficulties, as they paraphrased my mother's words: "No dejaban de llevarme con curanderas, doctores y especialistas porque no podía concebir."

One of the *comadres* in the pueblo, recalling my father's frustration with the delay of my mother's pregnancy, emphasized, "Yep, they wouldn't stop taking her to healers, doctors, and specialists. But she couldn't get pregnant, so they had to do something. ¿Qué no?"

"When are they starting a family? Didn't they get married to have children? What are they waiting for?" others queried as they involved themselves in things that were not their affair.

¿Qué les importaba? It was none of their business.

Talk didn't come just from the folks in town, however.

Some say that my father, in his eagerness to prove his manhood, started and spread these rumors. Many claimed that he boasted, "Marriage is for two things: to have boy children and to be served."

Finally Father Time gave way to Mother Nature, despite my father's frequent *bracero* absences. *Con la voluntad de Dios*—through God's goodwill, Alejandrina became pregnant.

I was born in 1948. Delivered in the home of my ancestors, I first saw the light of day in Tabasco. Soon I would become the smallest migrant in our family of three. However, it wouldn't be until much later that I would have to contend with the insecurity and pain of moving from one place to the next. That usually happened when the season or Juan's madness took us from one strange place to another with just the clothes on our backs.

Border Crossings

Tía Luisa, may she rest in peace, told me that after crossing the border I almost drowned. According to her, my mother was carrying me in her arms when she tripped and I fell into a water canal. Tío Magdaleno fished me out of the irrigation ditch. Tía claimed this was a sign that I was destined to live a long life in *el norte*. I, *la mojadita*, would forever be tied to the United States.

They say I was made in Texas but born in México. My family claims I was conceived during my mother's earliest visit to Weslaco, deep in the Valley of South Texas along the U.S.-Mexico border, when my father worked as a *bracero*.

Certain I would be a firstborn son, people claim that when my mother was eight months pregnant, my father sent her back to México to have me. A true nationalist and a patriot, he wanted *el primer hijo que nunca tuvo* to be born in Tabasco, Zacatecas, the place of his birth.

"Tú padre siempre deseó un primer hijo," one of my *tías* would often volunteer, reminding me that I had not been his first choice for a child.

To his surprise, I was born.

He never let me forget I was a girl. He never forgave me for it.

Other relatives say that my first contact with the United States was when I was three months old. Continuing their movement back and forth, my family lived in Weslaco. This was when Tía Luisa and her husband Magdaleno came to work in the fields with my father; Mother and I returned to be with him.

The way they recall it, all crossed the Rio Bravo safely. No one was arrested. No one drowned.

South Texas became my sometimes home. Sixteen months younger than I, my sister, Mague, was born there. Tabasco became my haven.

Woman Alone

She married him for life; instead, she became *una esposa de lejos*, a long-distance widow, when father became enamored with the illusion of *el norte*. After 1946, when he first signed on as a *bracero*, my father was as good as gone. It was then that his dreams became my mother's loneliness.

After life in the United States, he could no longer tolerate the life of a landed peasant. And he stayed away. He made no apologies. He gave no excuses. He had bigger dreams. Don't think they included my mother and me. From then, she had a marriage on hold that came alive only when my father showed up to rekindle my mother's lonely heart and to get her pregnant with yet another girl.

Were it not for Mother's insistence and Abuelo's pressure, Amá and I wouldn't have gone to South Texas to join him, where she stayed long enough to get pregnant and have my first sister, Mague.

Only child born when he was around was Mague. The rest of us were born in the home of his birth, away from him. Didn't care to return. Didn't want to be disappointed with the birth of yet another girl.

Soon, with a new infant in tow, he sent us back. Claimed life became too difficult. It was hard to maintain a growing family of four. Declared his dollars went further in México. As an obedient and loving wife, my mother followed his command. What he failed to confess was that not having a wife gave him the freedom to stray and to continue his womanizing ways.

She didn't seem to mind having him away, though. She accepted Father's absence as a consequence of her luck and lived with the choices she had made. Never complained.

Living near her in-laws, Mother seldom lacked for company or support, most of it from women. The only men in our midst were neighbors who were too young, too sick, or too feeble to follow the same migration path.

Many a time I heard their debates about Father's commitment to Amá. They commented on his stupidity for leaving such a beautiful and wonderful wife so far away.

"¡Qué tontería!"

"Que se cuide Méndez."

"Women like Alejandrina are hard to find."

"He should be concerned."

"Even with her girls Alejandrina would have no problem finding someone."

Because they knew her loyalty and devotion to him, few of these comments were made in her presence. But I heard them.

Mother never lost her figure. She grew more beautiful with each one of her births. Although her brood was expanding, every child she had gave her more patience and made her more attractive. She was kind. Had a great sense of humor. Loved to tease and to play around with us. Smelled of lemon blossoms. She was such a fine cook that relatives made excuses to come around when she was preparing any one of the three meals of the day. Known for her handmade corn *tortillas* and her roasted *chile verde* made in a mortar grinder, she drew them like flies to our kitchen.

A hard worker and a thrifty person, Mother made sure we never lacked for anything. And, I might add, because of her way with money, Amá made sure we fancied ourselves rich.

Mother was a loving and concerned parent who made sure all our needs were met. Because I was interested in learning, she stretched her budget to enroll me in parochial school, where I thrived. She was so proud of me; she often attended events and helped with whatever she could. She was invested in us, almost like a parent who tries too hard to fill the void of the absent father, wanting to be both.

Father's relatives accepted her as their kin and loved her. This often made him jealous. They took her in, protected her, loved her, and resented Father for leaving us behind. I assumed she suffered without him by her side, although she never said so.

Ahead of her time, she did not believe in hitting or spanking as discipline. Even Felisa, who could be a handful, found Mother's creativity and kindness when she found herself in time-out for her mischief. Mother had learned that keeping Felisa from her friends was a good way to keep her out of trouble. Mague and I were well-mannered and behaved. We gave her no problems. We loved to help her. She often said we were *bién acomedidas,* helpful.

Life with Mother was idyllic. Outside the everyday happiness with her, there is little else worth remembering. With Mother in our lives, my sisters and I had no time to miss our father.

No one could have guessed that her life with a dream husband would turn into a nightmare.

Ꙩ Pueblo de Tabasco

Leaving her husband behind and pregnant with Felisa, my mother took us girls back inside the smaller leg of *el jorobado.* That's what we called Zacatecas because its boundaries were drawn in the form of a hunchback. We were back in Tabasco. Life in the United States had been more difficult than my father had supposed.

In Tabasco, El Camino Real of the Spanish conquerors runs north. My ancestors traveled to San Antonio and other parts of the Southwest, searching for land and riches, just as my grandfather and father later would. *Vireinato de Zacatecas* supplied people and resources. Southeast is the path the Mexicas took to Tenochtitlán, once the glorious capital of the Aztecs.

Above Tabasco is Chicomoztoc, where the Mexicas began to construct the empire they envisioned after sighting the eagle perched on a cactus with the snake in its beak. Building stopped when their high priests envisioned the lake as the foundation of their city.

Surrounded by mountains, Tabasco is in a small valley where the climate remains the same year-round—never too hot and never too cold, just right. Father's family has lived there since it was founded. No one recalls when that was. Méndezes have always lived and owned property in Tabasco. All have had their *casitas*.

Huache. Mesquite. Temachaca. Words of trees.

Nopales. Tunas. Pitallas. Words of fruits.

Quelites. Verdolagas. Acualaistas. Words of greens and seeds.

Nourishing words. They still slide from my tongue. Words and tastes I miss that can still make my mouth water with just a thought.

Grown in Tabasco, as were my sister Felisa and I, sprouts from the *huache* and *temachaca* trees, in any form, were best of all. Sometimes *temachaca* was served as *caldo,* and the *huache* seeds were rolled inside corn tortillas with *chile.* Those were our favorite foods. They live in our memories and in our hearts.

Temachaca and *huache*—they must have cured our intestinal worms; nothing could have survived the gas they gave. The stench produced after eating them was our favorite part—got us kicked out of the best and worst places.

Mesquite pods that tasted like a pasty mix of sugar cane and licorice were our wild candy. We savored their sap and their seasons.

Caldo de temachaca, made with the new sprouts from the tree, was a great staple for Lent, as were *nopales* and *verdolagas*. *Tortas de camarón en mole o caldo*, powdered shrimp, made into patties served in chile gravy or as soup, replaced fish. *Capirotada*, here called bread pudding, the coveted *postre* of Semana Santa, survived in our recipes for Holy Week.

Pitallas, fruits from the *pitallo* cactus tree, that produced only once a year in the waning days of May, created a longing year-round. Mouth-watering, savory taste of prickly pears, with the feel of kiwi fruit without the tartness and the fuzz, is how I remember them. Bright colors: magenta, purple, red, and yellow-orange. Round shape with sparse light bristles, like growth on a pubescent boy's face. Some prolonged their final days for the promise of its taste. Abuelo Haro, my friend's grandfather, died with the word *pitalla* on his lips.

I lived off the land and loved being of the land.

Tatemadas, childhood memories of corn, corn cooking on the cob in its own husks on cinders of mesquite wood. We sisters still try to match the sweetness and taste of that corn of long ago.

All sorts of greens year-round gave life.

Tabasco gave me a penchant for vine-ripened tomatoes. None are better. I still seek them to recreate the taste of *salsa* and *chile verde*, as we had when I was a child.

In Tabasco, oregano, cilantro, and *yerba buena* gave me an appreciation for fresh herbs. I also learned to value scallions and onions of other colors, including leeks.

King-size *guayabas y aguacates* among the fruits grown there—no gua-camole ever tasted the same with its creamy, pungent, lemony tastes. *Guayabas* wrapped in a deep yellow, thin skin; their pink flesh satisfied even the sweetest tooth. The seeds were a nuisance with which we could deal. Later they became a memory for which we ached.

Aguacates were creamy and tasty with the texture of butter. We some-times savored their black, shiny, and delectable skin with the pulp spread inside our homemade corn tortillas. Didn't even need salt. Other times we added diced tomatoes, onions, chile, and cilantro—*pico de gallo* gave our *taco* the perfect touch. *Guayabas* and *aguacates* like those will never be had again—haven't had any that compare.

In Tabasco, food was available year-round—milk from the cows or goats, eggs and meat from the chickens—which I relished, except when I had to wring the chosen chicken's neck. This left the chicken doing a headless dance that took my appetite away. I didn't even eat meat for days. Just looking at the chicken made me sad.

I didn't know poverty or hunger. We lived off the land in Tabasco.

Robachicos among Us

Everybody knew everybody in my *pueblito de Tabasco*. It was a safe place where children could roam freely.

However, even in play, there were limitations. Our parents controlled our movements, putting the fear of gypsies and Huichol Indians in us, *con los gitanos y huicholes*. They were cast as *robachicos*, child stealers, and we children learned to suspect anyone who dressed in *huichol* or gypsy garb.

Didn't see it then, but we were just as Indian. Sadly, we were learning to fear ourselves.

In raw cotton the color of corn *masa*, wearing peasant pants and shirts embroidered in vibrant colors, adorned by multicolor ribbons, they came. The *huicholes* came down the mountain to sell their arts and crafts and to celebrate *la Virgen*. They wore *huaraches* and a colorful hat with a small rim decorated with dingle balls and ribbons. Their hats stood apart from those worn by the local peasants and workers. We'd learned to recognize them and stood ready to run and warn others of their presence in our midst. Their women seldom came to town.

Somewhat exotic, *gitanos* looked like long-lost cousins returning from an enchanted land. Men, women, and children wore colorful scarves on their heads. Sometimes the men donned a hat over them. The women wore gypsy blouses with supple, ankle-length, colorful skirts. Shimmering in their shiny adornments, they arrived. The jingling of their jewelry and the clanging of the horse-drawn buggies warned us of their presence.

They spoke funny Spanish and were overly friendly. We were warned to stay away.

"¡Correle! ¡Ahí vienen los huicholes! Run. The *huicholes* and the gypsies are coming!" residents yelled in fear as they rushed to warn others. When we saw them coming, we would fly home. Left the town empty. Until someone reported them gone. "Ya se fuerón. Salgan a jugar. They left. Go out and play," brought cheering as children went about their day.

Gitanos and *huicholes* were not the only ones used to control our activities. *El Cacarizo*, so called because of the pockmarks on his face from smallpox, also became a deterrent from lying.

"Sí me dices mentiras, te harás como el Cacarizo. Your face will grow pockmarks if you tell me lies, just like the *cacarizo*," Tía Herme would often warn us when she suspected we were fibbing. "Cada marca que tiene en la cara es una mentira. Every mark on his face records one of his lies. You better not lie to me, unless you want to look like *el Único.*"

Their stories worked for a while.

Despite the fear, we could go anywhere in our *pueblito*. We felt safe. It was comfortable. In Tabasco, pebbled, paved, wide streets provided safety for those who walked barefoot, willingly or out of necessity.

To the east of our town stood Villa del Refugio Catholic Church. That was where marriages, baptisms, confirmations, and last rites took place. Built in the Baroque style, our church was the gray color of the local granite and had a somber and sad look to it. Only the flowers and the greenery made it stand out from other buildings. Inside, color reflected the evangelical messages of purple, green, red, and white displayed to stir the emotions found in Bible stories. Purple was tied to the suffering of Jesus during Semana Santa.

A marble baptismal bath sat in the center. In that spot many in our pueblo must have been saved from damnation.

However, nothing could have saved our parish priest. People claimed he had a *señora* to "take care of his needs." She bore many children who looked like the priest and had no father. Knowing that the *señora* tended to more than the sacristy made the men feel comfortable about their wives' involvement with the church. This kept the *padre* away from their women.

It must've given them some comfort to know that even priests were sinners, as it gave others license to sin.

Saints from the motherland, what the priests called Spain, took their place in different sections of the church. There was a holy hierarchy. The altar was reserved for a bloody Christ figure on the cross. The only time he was displaced was December 12, the day of the Virgen de Guadalupe. St. Joseph stood on the right of the crucifix. Mother Mary, as a Guadalupe, on the left. *Santos* spread throughout the walls of Villa del Refugio. Iron and brick walls gated the church, and a pepper tree stood in the farthest corner at the front. Two steeples rose to the sky, making our church the tallest building in town. It had a bell tower in the middle. It looked like others built by Indians.

We never missed Sunday service. Always the first ones there, ready to show off our new clothes, made by Tía Herme, with material sent from the United States by our parents or bought in Tabasco with *los dólares* they sent. We made our communions and wore dresses designed by Tía. Never missed confession. We received the Holy Host every Sunday.

On the west side of the Plaza, across from the church, was el Palacio Municipal de Tabasco. The building stood at attention, like a guard, ensuring that the Catholic priests kept their noses out of the state's affairs.

Stores, *cantinas*, and restaurants filled the north and south sides of the center of town. We had only one hotel. Not many visited. Few stayed there, choosing instead to visit in relatives' homes—to save money.

North or south, east or west, the streets of Tabasco followed the four directions, like a pie with a center point. All points joined at the Plaza.

The Plaza Central, in the center of town, was Tabasco's heart. Nights and weekends, the Plaza became a *fiesta*.

Sundays were special at the Plaza. Many courtships began there.

Geraniums, roses, and calla lilies surrounded the *kiosko*. It came alive with the sounds of guitars or accordions, as *ranchera, norteña y música romantica* played from nearby bars. Built with white and red brick and iron gates for décor, *el kiosko* became more alive when it housed musicians who came to serenade the Tabasqueños. Live music brought everyone there. The Plaza was so packed that we felt like tamales in a cooking pot.

La Plaza and Its Surroundings

The Plaza had a life of its own. In the traditional dance of courtship, men and women promenaded in opposite directions, facing each other as they walked. Dressed in Sunday best—Western boots, buckles, hats, and blue jeans—suitors hoped to find love.

Averting direct eye contact, *los pretendientes* discreetly sized up each other. Eventually facing one another, they began the dance of romance.

Chaperones kept an eagle eye, making sure everything was done the proper way. Touching was off limits. Young women were forbidden from going anywhere without younger sisters or brothers hanging at their side.

Sometimes a *mordida* worked—bribes sent little ones away. Later, the youngsters would hold the couple hostage for more. With stories to tell, *escuincles* could reap big profits. I know. I was one of them.

Courtship at the Plaza was for everyone. Even *viudos* and *viudas* found their second mates there.

The pueblo's womanizers were known for taking *tacos de ojo,* as their eyes feasted on someone else's prospects. Sighing and commentary were their only consolation.

"¡Ay que curves, y yo sin frenos!"

To no one in particular and without restraint, men howled their appreciation for the curvy figures of the women who passed, lamenting their lack of brakes for the curves ahead.

"Psssst. Psssst."

Others called out for attention. They often threatened imaginary suicide, just to get a response.

"Pssst. Pssst. Mamacita, ven pa' aca. Pssst. Pssst. Ay qué si no me miras, me voy a matar."

"Pos te doy un cuchillo y te vas más pronto, pendejo. ¿Qué no?"

Insulted by the fool's comments, any one of the young women would have handed him a knife so he could follow through with his threat. This remark often received the laugh of the night.

"Con una mirada me manda al cielo," some innocent soul dared tell my cousin.

"A look from you, *pendejo*, will make me puke instead of send me to heaven. If you don't shut up, I'll give you a slap that'll send you straight down to hell," my cousin Choco answered.

"Pinches, ofrecidos." The responses didn't need a translation. It was the ultimate retort to the vulgarities of the *sinvergüenzas* who so shamelessly offered themselves.

These nightly pursuits created a spectacle for us. People-watching became our theater and the Plaza our stage.

Lover boys were not alone. They had reinforcements.

Like soldiers of Eros, food vendors set up shop around the Plaza, serving the appetites of the hungry and lovelorn. Attempting to make points, courting *novios* bought all types of tacos for those who guarded their intended target. *Tacos de tripas, lengua, carne asada y carnitas* were but some of the options. With the hope of a goodnight kiss, most men refused onions in their tacos. Young women asked for extra dollops, reinforcing chastity with onion boundaries.

Varieties of fruits, splashed with lemon and sprinkled with *chile*, and other special treats also enticed the senses in exchange for silence. They gave suitors a head start in making points for the wooing contest. They acted rich and spent half their wages buying complicity or *cariño*.

As for my sisters and me, accompanied by one of our *tías* or under my supervision, we were allowed to go to the Plaza so long as we returned before dark.

One of those nights I saw Tía Sara, my father's youngest sister and our charge to chaperone, accept Lionzo's overtures. That was the first time I tasted pineapple with *chile y limón*, my *mordida* for looking away. Two years later they married in the town church, and I was the proud flower girl. The taste of pineapple and *chile* reminds me of them.

Witnessing. Listening. This is how we learned about life.

Our *noticias* came from the Plaza. This was our dependable source of news.

Most evenings the *comadres* and friends gathered there, awaiting the responsibility of passing the word. Having no newspapers, we found that *chisme* was our lifeline.

When the government finally decided to provide electricity and running water, we heard about it at the Plaza. As expected, the *comadres* passed the word to the homebound. It was there I first learned that Cousin Concha was pregnant by Don Pablo. He came to install *agua potable*. According to the *comadres*, he laid his waterpipe in more than the town streets.

In the busy mouths of the Plaza, the family was scandalized. Concha marked her family and the town with shame.

Don Pablo, a Zapotec Indian from Oaxaca, was twenty years older than Concha. The anger wasn't over the age difference or because she became pregnant (she wasn't the first and wouldn't be the last); it was because *un indio la engañó*, an Indian duped her.

After word of her pregnancy became public, Concha and Don Pablo had a quickie marriage at Villa del Refugio. They moved away with his next assignment. That was the last time I saw Concha.

La Culebra: The Snakewoman

On the seedy side of the Plaza, we found other stories. To this day I'll never forget the time I went looking for *la Culebra*. She, along with *la Rosa*, were the town prostitutes. I was around six, but I knew who they were and what they did.

These *mujeres de la calle* hung out across from Villa del Refugio, sauntering back and forth until someone stopped to talk to them. Dressed in deep purples, pinks, and oranges, they made sure they stood out among the colors adorning the walls of the businesses that lined the Plaza. They didn't want to blend in; they wanted to stand out, to fill the space of their open-air business.

My friends from school had been making fun of me because my father, on his most recent visit, was seen about town with *la Culebra*. The townsfolk knew him as a *mujeriego*, a skirt chaser.

As little as I was, I was embarrassed for my mother. As his daughter, I felt humiliated.

Still, I tried to ignore those who made fun of me. That worked for a while.

But the day came when I could no longer take it. I went in search of *la Culebra*.

At the Plaza I camped out and waited for the woman whose Christian name was María. I awaited the evil woman who was chasing the wedded husband of my mother. I didn't know exactly what I would say, but I wanted her to stop upsetting my mother.

Then I saw her.

Strutting, she came toward me. She wore a bright red dress with a *chichi*-exposing neckline and high heels that *pinged* when they hit the cobblestone pavement. Her hair was long and hung below her waist as if to emphasize the crack on her back. She had an innocent look that reminded me of the face Felisa had the day she "found" a $20 bill at the base of Tía's cash register. Didn't buy Felisa's story. Didn't believe *la Culebra*'s innocence either.

Wherever she went, she turned heads. With her strut she became the fantasy woman every man wanted, including my father. Without the burden of their children, although she had plenty of her own, María tended to their lustful whims.

"Mira, ¡tu novia!" The men whispered to each other loud enough for her to hear. "Look. Here comes your girlfriend!"

She ignored them. Continued walking as if she owned the town.

La Culebra had no idea I expected her. She ambled in my direction with that calculated slither, making a curvy letter *s* as she walked. It was then that I heard myself whisper, "Leave my father alone. Don't chase after him. Don't you know you're hurting my mother?"

"¿Qué dijiste?" Asking what I had said, she continued walking.

I followed her, restating my concern.

"¡Dejelo! No sea mala."

I meant it. She ignored me. Pretended not to hear.

La Culebra walked past me, without even bothering to look my way. I didn't merit a look from her.

Then, with a voice that sounded like her walk, she hissed, "Yo no los busco. Son ellos los que me buscan."

She made it a point to tell me they sought her. They chased her.

As quickly as she appeared, she vanished without another word.

That was the end of *la Culebra*.

Don't know if she stopped messing with my father, but my friends stopped teasing me after that.

Mother never complained. She was too afraid of him or too in love. Didn't know the difference. They seemed to be one and the same to me.

Amor de su corazón

"Amorcito Corazón," Dearest Heart, will forever be their song. When she sang it, he was with her. She adored my father.

I never could understand why she loved him so. She missed him.

In her marriage my mother went back and forth between México and the United States. And she did all she could to be with him, trying to bring our growing family together.

Back in Tabasco, having left my father in South Texas, she never tired of showing her deep love for him. He was her everything.

It was different for me. As he had hardly been a part of my young life, I didn't know him. I don't even know if I liked him.

With his absence my father became the fairy-tale husband she longed to have. It must have been easy to love him more from afar.

In my mother's love for music, he became her Pedro Infante, singing a song I'll never forget.

> *Amorcito Corazón*
> *Yo tengo tentación.*

Dearest heart, I hunger for your kiss. In her voice, these words were a symphony she emphasized with that lively whistle. She sang it over and over again like a rosary that wouldn't end—*una plegaria de amor.* Sometimes her whistle alone was a call for his love.

She wished she could be with him. She longed for him.

When she sang their song, words slid from her lips like kisses in the wind. I imagined her losing bits of her heart—"Amorcito Corazón."

After almost eight years of separation, she went to live with him in the United States.

Finally her dream had come true. But ours was destroyed when she left.

Mague, Felisa, and I were left behind to live with our great-*tías.*

In *el norte* she worked the fields alongside Juan. Followed him to Chicago and other paths north. Gave up her family, her country, and her land. Chose him over the comforts of home. He was everything to her. She adored him.

For me, Juan was but a dream inside my mind. Only thing I had were photographs to remind me of his looks.

Married to my mother since 1945, his initial trip to the United States was before their first wedding anniversary and two years before I was born. He chose the easy life of *el norte* instead of harvesting his own land. Most men who went to the United States did it out of desperation, but for him it was adventure that called.

Without my father we lived with our mother surrounded by women—*tía abuelas, tías,* and others who had also lost their husbands to *el norte.* Those days were like living under the wings of a mother hen—warm, secure, comfortable, and loving.

One time my mother was away, and the tent cinema came to town. That's when I saw *Nosotros los Pobres.* Pedro Infante sang my mother's song, "Amorcito Corazón."

And I fell in love, too.

Pepe el Toro, the poor carpenter with the heart of gold, played by Pedro Infante, became the imagined father I never had. After this, I had no need to be with my own.

Que se entrega en el calor

A love given in the heat of our great love, my love—"Amorcito Cor-azón." I could hear my mother whistle the words; it made it easier for me to see her as Chorreada, the wife of Pepe el Toro. Loyalty and blind love for their man is what they both had in common. That's when I realized that "Amorcito Corazón" was a testament to my mother's love for Juan.

Singing their song, I imagined my mother wearing her '50s black skirt with white *concha* swirls and a nylon blouse with rhinestones and see-through short sleeves. She smelled of Ivory soap and Ponds face cream. I wanted her with us.

> Dearest heart
> I hunger for a kiss
> *Que se entrega en el calor*
> *De nuestro gran amor—mi amor.**

When she was with us, the song made her happy and angry all at the same time. I wondered how she felt now.

I never would have left my mother the way he did. Couldn't under-stand why she followed him.

The movie and her song let me pretend I was with her, if only for a moment. Luscious in her movie star housewife clothes instead of scummy like the name implied, it was easy for me to imagine being Chorreada and Pepe el Toro's daughter, Chachita. Chunky, *cachetonas*, big cheeks, with long braids, and the typical bib dress of the times—I fit into the role. I could be with Amá when I became Chachita.

Pepe el Toro was the father of my dreams who never left us.

* That's given in the passion / Of our great love—my love.

In my mind he stayed and loved my mother. He made all her romantic wishes real. He played the loving and caring father I had always wanted.

> Companions in good and bad
> That years cannot take away
> Dearest heart, you forever will be my love.

I imagine my mother singing their song of love. With the melody comes the confusion of being left behind like an off-key note jarring the romance. It reminds me of the time she chose him over her girls.

Bewitched by love, even as a young girl, I understood loneliness.

Chiquilladas

Didn't miss him. Missed my mother, but had my *tías*. They loved and took care of my sisters and me. We had school and her memory. We needed nothing more.

In school, teachers like Rosita, Lupe, and Arnulfo turned learning into play. It was a contest to solve math problems inside my head. Pencil and paper were for wimps. I practiced speeches good enough for presidents. Memorized, recited, and acted poetry. Danced *folklórico* and *flamenco*.

"¡Nunca se sabe cuando venga el presidente!"

Rosita would often remind us that the president of México could come through at any time. We had to be ready.

Sure enough, in 1959 I declaimed poetry for Presidente Arnulfo Ruíz Cortines when he came to Tabasco. Recited poetry and danced with Agustín Lara—my third cousin, not the world-famous composer of Mexican songs.

Created *artes manuales*—learned to sew, embroider, knit, and crochet, along with making pottery, paintings, and sculptures. School was never boring. There was no way I would have missed it.

A three-room adobe building, with a patchy field of grass *cancha* to play soccer or *beísbol*, our school was on the outskirts of Tabasco. I learned to ride a rented bike in its yard. Played tag, hide-and-seek, and games of early school days. Sang songs like "Víbora de la mar":

> *A la víbora, víbora de la mar, de la mar*
> *por aquí pueden pasar los de adelante*
> *corren mucho y los de atras*
> *se quedarán tras, tras, tras.**

Each word slithered from our lips, as the snake line passed underneath the arms of those whose hands framed the bridge that kept some in and let others out. Fun things happened there. But life in Tabasco wasn't all joy; I also lived with the fear of my father's visits.

Belting

Fear and Father were the same to me.

I had always been afraid of my father. Never feared the devil as much as I feared him. Seldom looked forward to his returns. My father didn't even compare to my ideal, Pedro Infante.

What others would say, *el que dirán*, was very important to my father. He carefully protected his position and his public reputation.

How he looked was important to him. *Bién planchado. Almidonado.* Dressed in rolled-up *norteamericano* jeans and a plaid cowboy shirt, he walked around as if he owned the town, splashed in Aqua Velva.

Mother faded into the stucco when he was present.

When he came back, she turned into a wallflower. He became the sun around which her life revolved.

* Of the snake, snake of the sea, of the sea / those in the front may pass through here / 'cause they're running a lot / and the ones in the rear / will stay behind, hind, hind, hind.

It was a September day when my father returned to México. Usually, his visits meant *borracheras*. Known as a mean drunk, he thought his dollars could get him out of any fix. "Tengo muchos dolares de los yunaitis."

When anybody tried to stop him, he would say, "I'll fucking drink if I feel like it. I have money. Lots of U.S. dollars. No jodan. Es mi pinche gusto tomar. Larguense."

One day during his visit, I went to look for him at the *cantina*. I don't remember why. My mother must have sent me to get him.

As a five-year-old girl, I went barefoot and put my father's good name up for ridicule. I entered the *cantina*. He looked straight at my bare feet, while pretending not to notice. Didn't realize until then that I looked like what he most detested: *una India, pata rajada*. By the look in his eyes, I knew I was in for it—I had shamed him with my bare Indian feet.

Too frightened to go home, I went to Tía Herme's. I hoped he wouldn't find me. But I knew what awaited.

He came looking for me. Petrified, I just stood there.

Glaring in my direction and moving toward me when he saw me, he pulled out his belt in one quick swoop. Handed it to me. Told me to soak it in the *tina*. A wet leather belt hurts more and leaves no traces.

Shaking, I did what he told me. I knew better than to disobey him, but I took my time following his command.

"¡Josefina!" he screamed in a drunken stupor. "¿Qué esperas, chingada muchacha?" "What the fuck are you waiting for?" he repeated. Trembling in fear, I imagined this was not happening to me. But I knew better, because this was not the first time he had hit me.

"¡Sí, Papá!"

Slowly walking toward him, I handed him the soaking wet belt.

"¡Cómo que, Papá! Chingada muchacha. ¿Qué no tienes zapatos?"

"Sí. Pero quería andar descalza."

He mocked my bare feet. I just wanted to feel the earth between my toes.

With every slap of the belt, pleasure shone in his eyes.

The scent of alcohol and Aqua Velva made my stomach turn. I felt as if he was never going to stop.

Whoosh. He hit my legs.

"Ésto es para que sepas que ningún hijo mio me avergonzará."

Smack. There went my back.

"Ésto es para que no andes descalza."

Splat. He almost hit my face.

"Que nunca más se te ocurra andar sin zapatos. ¿Me entiendes?"

The slaps of the belt and his words emphasized that no child of his would shame him by walking barefoot. To stress his point, he told me not to ever get the idea that I could walk without shoes, and he continued hitting me. Each word stung deeper than the welts from his belt. He did not want an Indian for a daughter.

Soon, the belt became a slithering snake that came alive with the venom of his blows.

"All that for not wearing shoes?" my shaking, aching, and sobbing body seemed to say. "For walking barefoot?"

It was with that one blow when I hit the cobblestone patio at Tía Herme's, when I faced the ground, that he finally stopped. He had ripped a toenail from my left foot. The splattering of blood made him stop.

"¡Vete a comprar zapatos! ¡Chingada muchacha!"

Tía Herme finally heard the commotion; she came to my defense. Threw Juan out of her house, scolding him for having hurt me.

"¡Eres un animal! See what you've done!"

"¡Lárgate de aquí!"

He left.

I still carry the scar on the middle toe of my left foot. I have no toenail.

Saints and Revolutionaries

Tía Herme and Tía Chenda were the *santas y revolucionarias* who graced my life. They weren't saints because they performed miracles. They survived daily life. *Fueron santas porque sobrevivieron.* Also, among the women I adored was Genoveva. We called her Geno.

Tall and lanky, Geno, who lived across the street, *casi fue milagrosa.* Emitting a flowery scent that intoxicated, she dressed in black, wrapping her face and upper torso in the traditional *rebozo.*

Her home was a daily pit stop for me. On my way to school, I stopped by Geno's. Along with Chona, she was part of my day, unless I missed school. And that couldn't happen because Tía believed "my guts had to be coming out of my stomach" for my sisters and me to miss school.

Without fail I found Geno making her Nescafé. She gave me the *nata,* the layer of cream from her boiled milk, and made me a child-sized cup of light caramel-colored coffee. It was the best I have ever tasted.

With her ability to get around, she fascinated me. She could hear and sense things before anyone. Most of the time I didn't even have to knock; she was at the door before I arrived. Geno knew I was there just by the sound of my footsteps.

Her house was very dark. I could barely see inside the kitchen. So as not to trip or spill, I made every effort to stay by the door near her *saguán,* the entry to her house.

Geno made me feel like an equal. When I went to her house, I was just like any other adult who visited. She listened to me. She gave me so much attention that I thought Geno actually could see me.

She was independent and never asked for help.

She was our neighbor. Had no relatives.

Had no children. Never married.

Geno did not complain about her life. I marveled at how she managed. I don't know who supported her, but she made do with dignity and pride.

My *tías* Chenda and Herme were examples of revolutionary women. They were not *soldaderas.* They didn't fight in wars. They supported themselves as widowed women alone.

Both sisters had married *rancheros.*

Chenda married Rafael, whose last name I've never learned. He worked the land.

Herme wedded Don José Enciso, who raised cattle and tended the land they owned. *¡Don José Enciso era rico! ¡Rafael era pobre!*

When we—Mague, Felisa, and I—came into their lives, the widowed sisters, who never remarried, lived together. Chenda ran the home. She cooked. She cleaned. She washed. And she mended clothes for Herme, her young son, Pepe, and for us later in our lives.

Chenda was rail-thin and her pores exuded the spices of her cooking— smelled of cloves, oregano, black pepper, and garlic. Dressed in the somber colors of mourning, slightly hunchbacked and with a limp, Chenda wore a permanent bun on her head. She walked with a cane.

She was a gifted storyteller. But, more than that, Chenda was a cooking *curandera* whose stories came alive when she cooked the food that healed others.

"Pina, yo sobreviví la Revolución Cristera y la Revolución Mexicana," she repeated, using my childhood name. She had lived through the Mexican Revolution and the Cristero War between the Catholic Church and the state. She often told me how she survived both wars as she cooked steak for her clove-spiced *mole de Chona.* The Cristero War was more painful than the Revolution for her. As a good Catholic, Chenda resented the federal soldiers' attacks on the Cristero believers who had risen to protest the stripping of land and wealth from the Church after the Mexican Revolution.

"En el santuário mataron muchos," Chenda said almost to herself, as she recalled the war between the Catholic Church and the Mexican government. They killed many at the old sanctuary church, during an unforgettable weekend. State soldiers wanted to teach a lesson to the Catholics who rebelled, killing them on their own holy ground. She told me the story often enough to let me know that she didn't want to forget the life she had led. I'll always remember what she said.

> Durante la guerra Cristera, un federal, que tenía poca paciencia con aquellos que no veían las cosas como él, decidió liquidar a cada persona que no tuviera lealtad a la patria. Para anunciar la matanza, el federal mandó repicar las campanas del santuario. El campaneo que siempre trajo alegría y celebración ahora dejaba chillidos al anunciar la desgracia.
>
> Fue horrendo lo que pasó. Hombre tras hombre y mujer tras

mujer, fueron llevados a fuerza de bayoneta hasta la azotea del santuario donde los empujarón a su muerte. Caían gritando: "¡Qué viva Cristo Rey!"

Mataron tanta gente que la cantera frente al campanario se quebró. Por la sangre derramada, la banqueta color crema cambió a color rojo oscuro.

No fueron minutos—la matanza duró todo un fín de semana.

Cuando me tocó, resistí. Golpeada y con la cadera quebrada grite. "Todos seremos responsables por el río de sangre, al menos que paremos estas atrocidades."

Se rebeló el pueblo. Todo terminó cuando alguien liquidó al responsable. Cómo recuerdo me quedó esta chuecura.*

Chenda pointed at her mangled hip, the proof of her resistance to the mass killings that weekend long ago. She grabbed her walking stick and hobbled toward the stove to stir the *mole* she had so tenderly prepared.

Her stories always made me cry, but the aroma of her red *mole de Chona* filled me with life.

---

* During the Cristero War a federal official, who had limited patience for those who did not see things as he did, took it upon himself to liquidate every person whom he perceived to be disloyal to the nation. The official rang the Santuario bells to announce the killings. The ringing of the bell that had brought much joy and celebration in the past had an eerie sound like none previously heard. What took place was horrific. Man after man and woman after woman who refused to reject their faith were taken to the roof by force of the bayonet where they were thrown to their death, crying out, "Long live Christ the King!" They killed so many townsfolk that the stone broke where they stood. The ground changed from cream to a deep crimson red because of the blood that was shed. The killings did not last for minutes or hours; they lasted an entire weekend. When my turn came, I resisted. They beat me and broke my hip. Still battered, I screamed, "We will all be responsible for the river of blood that runs, unless we stop these atrocities." The people rebelled, and everything was put to an end. With my words I had convinced someone to kill the official who led the atrocities. I live with this limp as a reminder of those times.

As I ate the savory slivers of the mouth-watering steak in red *tomatillo* sauce with corn *tortillas*, *frijol de la olla*, and the best *sopa de fideo* ever, I wept at the possibility of not having had Chenda in my life.

⟳ Widowed by Lightning

Left in an empty bed, my *tías* lived alone the rest of their lives. They must have loved their men enough to remain by themselves, despite interested suitors. They had a hard life, a lonely, loveless life. Cuco Sánchez's "Cama de Piedra" comes to mind when I think of the love my *tías* had for their husbands. It was a song they both loved.

> *De piedra ha de ser la cama*
> *De piedra la cabecera*
> *La mujer que a mi me quiera*
> *Me ha de querer de a deveras*
> *Ay, ay, corazón, por que no amas.**

Longing. They lived.
Suffering. They overcame.
Surrendering. They gave us love.

I learned from Chenda how they became widows—both sisters had been married to their husbands for less than two years. The whole town knew the story, but no one talked about it.

"Fue en el tiempo de lluvias."

Telling me that it was during the rainy season, my *tía* said, "Don José," Tía Herme's husband, "fue a protejer el ganado, rounded up the cattle. It

---

* Cuco Sánchez, the singer, sings about the difficulty of finding a woman who will love him, despite the hardships of poverty: Of rock will be the bed / Of rock the headrest / The woman who loves me / Will truly love me / Oh, oh, my heart, why don't you love me?

was something he did. He tended his own livestock because a proud man takes care of what he owns."

As she told me the story, I imagined the rainy season.

It is the most beautiful time of year, although Tabasco and its surrounding areas have beauty year-round. Everything is green and in bloom. Wildflowers of all colors come up everywhere. Purples, yellows, and reds of the *amapolas, sangre de Cristo, margaritas,* and other flowers with names I've forgotten, splashed the landscape. The wet earthen smell of the soil, like the fresh water served from a *jarrón de barro,* whetted our thirsts.

Thunder and lightning lit up the sky everywhere when it rained. Scared me. Kept us inside. Made the superstitious bring out the metal knives to protect their homes. They would go to every corner possible, and every space of entry, making the sign of the cross with a steel knife to cut the power of thunder. Didn't protect anyone outside the house, though. I don't think it protected anyone inside either.

Repeating what she had just said with the urgency of someone who has to tell her story, Tía Chenda continued. "Don José wanted to protect the livestock from harm. Hermelinda estaba criando a Pepe que apenas tenía tres meses."

As the mother of a three-month-old, Herme was worried about her husband in that weather. She tried to talk him out of going. But according to Chenda, "No hizo caso." He wouldn't listen.

The memory they shared in common was of Don José mounting his horse and riding away. Both sisters sent him on his way.

"¡Esa fue su muerte!" That was his death.

Rounding up the cattle, he was struck by lightning. Died on the spot.

No one would have guessed that lightning would unite the sisters forever. Tía Chenda's husband, Rafael, also lost his life that way in that same rainy season. Tending the same herd of cattle, he, too, was struck by lightning and perished on the spot, not too far away from where Don José lost his life.

Lightning sealed the sisters' fate. Their husbands' deaths united them for life. Neither married or desired to wed again.

Chenda moved into Herme's house to help care for her nephew Pepe.

Married poor and bearing no children, her choices were limited. She had nothing and was left with nothing. She lived with her sister until the very end.

With Chenda's help, Herme ran her *tiendita*, the storefront in front of her house, and she managed the land and cattle left by Don José. Together they saw Pepe through college and graduation from the university. He became a professor.

Then, together, they tended us. *¡Qué mujeres!*

Reading *Madrinas*

With only a second-grade education and the love of the written word, my mother taught me to read before I was three. I learned the vowels with her tale of *el burro*.

"Aaaaaa-a, eeeeeee-e, iiiiii-i, oooooo-o, uuuu-u . . . El burro sabe más que tú."

To please my mother, I mouthed each vowel as a talking donkey would, showing her I was smarter than the donkey. I was no *burra*. I made my mother proud.

"Aaaaaa-a, eeeeeee-e, iiiiii-i, oooooo-o, uuuu-u . . . El burro sabe más que tú."

But she wasn't my only reading *madrina*. I had others. Tía Herme was one; Chona, who owned the *novelas* and *vidas ejemplares* stand in Tabasco, was another.

Aside from the classroom, Chona's *puesto* was the only reading place in town. Her stand was in the northeast corner of the Plaza across from the *mercado*. On my way to the *mandado* to buy our groceries for the day, Chona's place was my first and last stop. Reading was my love.

The *mercado* came in a close second, though. Good food and reading could always win my attention.

Skipping along the way, the scent of fresh *manteca* and the just-cooked, crispy *chicharrones* and freshly made *carnitas* tickled my hunger. The sweet vanilla and the just-baked, sugary *pan dulce;* the prickly smell of *cebollitas verdes* and dirt red color of *rabanos;* and the fresh-cut flowers made my insides dance and sing. Even the buzzing flies that hung near the meat racks added spice to my chore. I stopped to witness the *moscas* draw a flurry of *maldiciones* from the *carnicero* as he heatedly shooed them out of his shop.

"Pinches moscas. Hijas de su . . . ¡Vayan a joder a otro lado!"

He made me laugh every time. Flies ignored him.

Didn't understand Spanish, I guess. But they scrammed in reaction to the swish of his fly swatter and his cussing—I would have, too. With a brain too small to keep the insult inside, though, the *moscas* quickly returned, hanging around as if they were idling planes ready to attack. They left only when shooed again, just to repeat the back-and-forth trip—hanging around was their job.

The *moscas*, my friends, and I did the same thing when chased by Tía and her fly swatter during one of our many reprimands.

I loved going to the *mercado.*

My day began with Tía Herme, who woke me with enough time to go to the market to visit Chona. This gave me time to enjoy reading before school started. Sharing my passion for books, Tía Herme hurried me along.

As I dressed, she called out the *provisiones* I had to get at the *mercado.* Had to get a half-kilogram of thinly sliced beef or a slab of meat, which the *carnicero* ground on the spot. Used it for the *guisos* or soups Tía Chenda made that day. Bought tomatoes, *chiles*, and onions for our salsas. Sticks of cinnamon for the coffee. Warm corn *tortillas* wrapped in brown grocery paper that turned sweaty and wrinkled by the time I got home. Purchased whatever fruit was the freshest, such as pineapple, mangos, sometimes bananas—unless they were black. Learned to pick the fruit. The pineapple had to have some green, and the middle of the stalk would have to easily yield a leaf if I pulled it. The mango had to be slightly hard when I palmed it. I was told not to squeeze it *porque lo mayugas*, I would bruise it. *Pan dulce—orejones, cochinitos, cemitas, pan de huevo.* My stomach jumped just hearing the names, but not as much as at the expectation of scanning Chona's books.

"Buenos días, Chona. ¿Cómo está?"

"Muy bién," she guided me to the new arrivals. I went through all the books, carefully looking for the new ones.

When I found nothing, I resorted to the aisle where Chona kept the *Santos y Santas de las Vidas Ejemplares*, the life stories of saints. There I looked for St. Francis of Assisi, saint and protector of animals. Sought St. Anthony, favorite of those who lost something and desired marriage or wanted to find love. Our Lady of Guadalupe, the miracle worker and saint of all causes and mother of the Americas, was always an option, but I knew her story by heart. The children of Lourdes, with secrets of salvation or world demise and models of goodness, would always do. I was nosy. Wanted to know what they kept secret. The Virgin of Fatima had told them of things to come. They knew when the world would end. I was curious. Wanted to dig up what I could. I found nothing. Only perfect kids.

Reading Veronica and Archie comics was always a consolation prize. Their American pranks were funny. But what they did was nothing compared to what my friends and I would try in our *pueblo*. A couple of times I dared to read *La Pequeña Lulú—era muy traviesa* and not of my *tía*'s liking. With her two finger curls standing up at attention, Lulú could always find ways to get into hot water, and we already had enough mischief with Felisa. When Lulú tried to fix her messes, she just dug herself deeper into them. Her *travesuras* were too *gringas* for us. Tía liked my reading the good books of saints rather than getting ideas from foreign *cochinadas*.

Because of my daily stops, I had read most of Chona's books. Lost track of the times I read *Santa Teresita del Niño Jesús*. But I couldn't forget that, like her, as *a buena niña católica*, I fended off a cousin who tried to abuse me. Teresita was killed in the process, giving up her life for her chastity. But I was not harmed, and I lived.

These stories of chastity and virtue, kindness, generosity, and protection were an inspiration. They taught me other lessons that were not as good—accepting my lot in life because I was a girl or obeying my father at whatever cost.

"Adiós, Chona. Ya me voy. Voy a llegar tarde a la escuela."

I was glad school didn't start until later that morning. It gave me time to read at Chona's.

Having visited many magical places on my way to the *mercado*, I had to get the *manteca* then rush back home to get ready for breakfast.

Strained in cheesecloth and spooned into paper that was folded, twisted, and sealed like an *empanada* to keep the lard in, the pork fat looked like watery mashed potatoes and it made a big spot on the paper bag. I had just enough *manteca* left to cook the eggs we would eat that day. Had I stayed longer, the lard could have seeped out, leaving a trail for the hungry animals that roamed. There wouldn't have been enough with which to cook.

As I left, Chona reminded me that I didn't need money to come to read because my credit was good.

"Sí, m'ija. Vuelva, aquí su crédito es bueno."

In our *pueblito* I learned much. Books were my life and life was my school. I learned new things even when I wasn't expecting to.

Dulce

Just back from their *luna de miel*, newlyweds Abuelito and Belén spent a few days visiting and slept on the extra bed in my bedroom. They went to bed with the chickens, forcing me to go to bed, too. One time after falling asleep, I was awakened by the creaking sounds of the coil springs.

In the moonlight I could see dancing shadows on the wall facing their bed. Stucco walls swayed with the sounds. Looking at the source of the ghosts, I could see the sheets waving with a mix of soft mooing and howling familiar to me but not connected to people: cows, dogs, and *coyotes* maybe, but not people.

Soon enough the noise and figures lost their appeal. I went to sleep.

In our home, like a *pension* that welcomed all who came, we had no privacy. Our beds were open to all guests. Available, just like the open-air outhouse we called *el corral*. Until that one day I went to the corral with my mother. I felt safe going with her. Then I saw something I never noticed before.

"Amá. ¿Qué es eso? Traí una araña por allá."

Scared, I yelled that she had a spider down there, between her legs.

"No, Josefina. No es una araña. Tan solo son pelitos. Es algo que viene con la madurez. ¡Ya verás!"

My mother explained that it was pubic hair. She also told me I would have it some day. Reassured, I felt no fear. I was satisfied with her answer.

After that, she never went to the corral with me. That's when I learned to value privacy. I also learned to be more careful with my expressions.

From that time on, whenever I went to the corral, I relieved myself like a lady. *En cuclillas*, squatting, I carefully arranged my skirt as I had seen my mother and other women relatives do. Now I knew what all those lifts, tucks, and folds meant. The trick was to raise my skirt or dress up in the back, just enough, without showing the crack. Folding the fabric and bringing it forward, I laid it on my lap so as not to wet or soil it. Sometimes I tented my skirt, making way for the yellow river up front.

No one ever had a peek at me. But we had our eyes peeled. We saw and heard many things.

Everything did it. Horses, cows, pigs, and goats got on and off as often as they liked. The rooster always had his choice of *gallinas* in the pen. The *burro* had a *pito* as big as my leg and just as thick. How could I not notice? We all did! Never saw the *burro* do it, because we had no *burras*. Only *burras* around were us girls when we did something wrong.

Good at being kids, we especially noticed things we were told not to see.

"¡No miren! Les van a salir perrillas."

Don't look! You'll get boils on your eyes. Our mothers taught us that watching dogs do it produced little volcanoes with a snowcap of pus on our eyelids.

How silly, as if looking at dogs doing it could make our eyelids pregnant with a puppy! How dumb!

"*Cochina*. What were you doing?"

Mothers were always ready to throw a bucket of cold water on the dogs when they caught them sniffing around each other's butt. Other times they tried to untangle the dogs, creating a circus for us to enjoy. If we hadn't seen it before, we sure noticed then. They had a long, thin *pito*.

Interesting. *Pito* and *chile* were used for people and animal things, and *pito* was even the word for a flute or whistle.

Chile, when used by grown-ups, seemed to mean more than a spice. *Papaya, pan y panocha*—fruit, bread, and brown sugar—were also names used for a girl's downthere. Young boys and dirty old men alike often talked about that sweet.

"All you have to do is go behind the counter. Let him touch you down there." She pointed to her *panocha*. "Then, he'll give you what you want."

Señor Landín, *el grosero* of the grocery, gave out candy.

My friend Guille told Rosa, Cielo, and me how easy it was to get it from him. Couldn't believe she would let him touch her *dulce*. We were not supposed to share our candy.

"No way! ¡*Cochina*! That's stupid!"

"You're letting him touch you down there? For candy?"

"¿*Saben qué*? I heard Doña Chencha tell the *padre* what she does to her husband and what he does to her while I waited for confession," Rosa piped in, changing the subject.

"¡Mentirosa!"

"You're such a liar."

"*La besa aquí, y le chupa allá*," Rosa said, pointing to embarrassing body parts, repeating that Doña Chencha had kissed here and touched there.

"There's more."

We were bored. Nothing new to learn. Had heard all that before.

We also played doctor with the boys. Cousin Jorge and his *ganga* liked to dare us to show our parts. He liked playing the doctor.

As luck would have it, he was the cutest of the bunch. Except for those of us who were related, all my friends dropped their *chonis* and let him look.

One even let him get close enough to see the *jetas,* lips. He wanted to see where her *pito* was. He was curious about where the *pipi* water came from.

We girls also had a turn. We asked only those who were as cute as Jorge to show their *cosas.* Boys had no problem dropping their drawers. The girls knew how and when.

We knew what happened with sex. You had babies. Still, some took risks.

Felisa and I would soon see our mother get pregnant. But that wouldn't happen until Amá had her first son. She had gone to be with him, again, and would soon return with a big belly.

¿A donde iran los muertos?

Quién sabe a donde iran

Where will the dead go?

Who knows where they will go

Our Homes

In my mother's absence, Tía Herme's home became our shelter—Mague's, Felisa's, and my refuge. When our mother left to join our father in Chicago, our newly remodeled house remained empty. Both homes became a symbol of our abandonment; neither one was really ours.

Felisa seemed to get over it soon. At Tía Herme's she sang, danced, or just plain acted on the top of the wide adobe fence that was her stage. Once, Felisa lost her balance and fell on her head. Didn't bleed or crack her skull. Just had the biggest *chipote* bump.

Tía's store was at the corner of her property, which took up almost a block on both sides. Her *tiendita* was stocked with canned, dried, and a few perishable goods. But the best part was the jar of *chiles jalapeños* marinated in vinegar with onion slices and carrots that never had time to go bad, because she sold them individually to children who enjoyed them with their saltine crackers or to *borrachos* who ate them with sardines. Felisa, the champion chile eater, was her best customer. She bought her *jalapeños* with money saved from her performances.

Evenings, Herme's store became a meeting place.

Bringing out the chairs, my *tías* and the neighbors sat and enjoyed talking about old times. Sometimes it would be the Revolution; other times they would just chew the *garra*—talking to talk. Had nothing else to do. They inspected their targets best when the chosen victims were not there. Those who went north, those who left their spouses, and those who stood outside the town's expectations were also easy targets.

The white stucco house stood out from the others because it was so public—a store and a home—but it felt like a cozy nest to me. Adorned with family pictures and portraits of saints we thought of as family, the walls were like a giant page in a history book. Generations of ancestors and saints watched over us. Besides the store, three more bedrooms completed the house. Herme's only son, Pepe, kept his room even when he was away at college. We often passed by it, but his room was off limits. We slept in the dining area, which became a long-term temporary bedroom for us girls. It was between Pepe's and Chenda's rooms, along with the *bañera* that housed a huge *tina* for bathing. We crossed the stone floor of the patio into the courtyard to get to the kitchen and to the earthen oven. But Chenda reigned over that space. It was very dark. Behind Chenda's realm was the corral where the livestock were kept. Didn't have an outhouse. Still did our business as an open-air affair but away from the *animales*, separated by a fence—didn't want the animals to eat our waste.

Herme's house was a menagerie of pets. She had four cats. *La tuerta*, who had lost her good eye in a cat brawl, was our favorite. With only the white of her blindness in one eye and a hole in the other, Tuerta was often the target of our *chiquilladas*. We loved to tease her. Moving chairs and tables around, we blocked her path and laughed when she bumped into something. The more confused and upset Tuerta became, the more we laughed.

Soon we grew bored, or our *tías* put a stop to our cruelty.

Replaced the furniture.

Our *gata* was safe again.

After our games, Tuerta stayed away for days. She'd run when she sensed us.

Eventually she'd forget our games and look for us. Then we would start the cat-and-mouse cycle all over again.

We never hurt her. Only wanted to play and have fun.

Wonder if she missed us like we longed for her, when we left for the United States.

The chirping and singing of birds filled the house like the morning *serenatas* our *tías* would get on their birthdays. Canaries, finches in the colors of the rainbow, and *sensontles* or larks occupied the space. Don Pedro Loro, an Amazon parrot with blazing colors of red, yellow, and blue, ruled above all. *Jaulas por donde quiera.* Birdcages filled the house. We woke to the morning songs of the birds.

Don Pedro Loro lived on the side entrance where water, wood, and store deliveries were made. Don Loro lived in a person-size iron cage in that *sagúan*, the passageway that led to the courtyard. He spoke better than the mayor, some joked. Cussed with conviction. Gave orders.

It wasn't unusual for Don Loro to allow entrance to vendors.

"Pase."

If they hesitated and knocked a second time, he resorted to more colorful language. "Chingaó. ¡Dije pase!"

Carefully closing the gate behind them, vendors left their deliveries, thinking someone authorized it. Of course, none were aware they were talking to a bird.

When they came to collect their payment, Tía protested, thinking they were overcharging.

"Mire, señora. Le traje leña y alguien me dió el pase."

"Tiene la boca peor que un arriero. ¡Me maldijo! ¡Me rayó la madre!"

After having delivered wood and being told to come in, the vendors complained about the gutter mouth that had given them the go-ahead. Claimed he had royally cussed them out.

Smiling, Tía Herme explained and paid the bill.

"My good man, that was a parrot who let you in. There are no men in this house. Must've been Pedro Loro."

Tía Herme always paid her bills. Even when Don Loro gave the go-ahead. Herme wouldn't take advantage of others. Expected the same in turn.

Felisa and I were Tía's other singing birds. Walking along and led by Felisa, our voices could be heard up and the down the streets as we made our way to school or to play with friends.

"Tu y las nubes" was Felisa's favorite song. We sang it like a broken record.

> *Tu y las nubes me traín muy loco*
> *tu y la nubes me van a matar*
> *yo p'arriba volteó muy poco*
> *tu pa' bajo no sabes mirar.**

* You and the clouds are driving me crazy / you and the clouds will be the death of me / I seldom look upward / and you don't know how to look beneath you.

Our street songs were a medley of unfinished pieces. We switched tunes as we forgot the words. Neighbors along the way would sometimes come out and clap or compliment us. Other times, the grouchy ones would scream for us to stop. Those who liked our songs would give us treats.

We must have done all right. No one ever splashed cold water in our direction, as they did with undesirable suitors who brought *mañanitas*.

Life was a daily *serenata*. We were its troubadours.

When three-year-old Felisa roamed the streets with Cousin Salvador or Licha, she felt free to stop at Ramón's *cantina*. Making a grand entrance, Felisa offered to sing in exchange for a soda—her code word for beer.

"Les canto una canción por una soda."

We had learned to say "soda" from our *gringo*-ized parents. Of course, the regulars got a kick out of her request, but Coca-Cola would be the only thing she was given.

Usually, the bartender, Ramón, would lift perky Felisa to stand her on the counter to sing her song. Dancing and swaying with the music, she'd belt out "Amorcito Corazón," our mother's love song. Encouraged by the applause and her Coca-Cola, she'd follow with "Que seas felíz," delivering a rendition worthy of María Victoria, the torch singer and star of Mexican movies. Groaning and sighing in the appropriate places, Felisa brought to life the nickname given to the Mexican singer: María *pujidos*.

> Que seas felíz, felíz, felíz
> es todo lo que pido de nuestra despedida
> en vez de despedirnos con reproches y con llantos
> yo que te quise tanto
> quiero que seas felíz, felíz, felíz.*

An encore would often get her sodas for the entourage. It was then that Felisa complied with a potpourri of her favorites, all of which she partially knew.

* May you be happy, happy, happy / is all that I ask of our farewell / instead of saying good-bye with resentments and with tears / I who loved you so much / wish you to be happy, happy, happy.

Impressed with her stage presence and her voice, the barflies tossed Felisa a few coins. Victorious, she would run to Tía's corner store and buy candies for all.

Felisa's performances were the talk of the town.

In our walks to or from school, sometimes we'd stop at Chito Lara's. He was known as *el doctorcito*. Our grandfather's cousin, we called him Tío Chito.

Chito wasn't really a doctor, but he could give injections and make *remedios*, deliver livestock, and cure animals. When people in the town couldn't afford to pay Dr. Nacho López or when he was too busy to see them, they went to Chito Lara. He never sent anyone away.

Tío Chito was a happy and friendly person. Some say his *remedios*—a mixture of ethyl alcohol and strawberry or orange soda—made him that way. Still other townsfolk swore that his sodas were his downfall.

"¡Se volvió loco!" Went crazy!

Tío wasted away from his own cures, dying of liver problems with no recollection of his life. Couldn't even remember his name.

Agustín Lara, his son, was my dance partner. We danced *flamenco* on Tuesdays and Thursdays.

Wearing a red dress with white polka dots, with a short train in the back and long fitted sleeves, draped in a *mantilla*, with my dance shoes on, I bounced along with the clicking of my castanets, propelled by the joy of the dance. Showing off. Displaying my attire for all to see.

Felisa often followed me to dance class.

Too young to be part of it, she paid close attention, and she copied all the steps. When my teacher would compliment us, Felisa would clap. She was our number one fan, our loyal audience of one.

"Ustedes son los mejores. Se miran muy monos."

Rosita told Agustín and me that we were the best and the cutest, as we practiced to the songs of Lola Flores, *la faraóna*. But Spanish dances weren't the only thing I studied. I also learned *las alteñitas, el jarabe tapatío, las chiapanecas, las bicicletas,* and other Mexican dances.

Loved twirling and swirling in my Jalisco costumes.

But what I loved best was getting lost in the yards of colorful and frilly fabric of those dresses that Tía Herme made with so much love.

"Prestame las enaguas. Yo quiero bailar."

Felisa would beg to borrow my dance outfits as she jumped around me like a Jack Russell puppy, yelping that she knew the dances. She wanted to practice them.

"¡Mira! Yo me las se. Dejame practicar. ¿Qué no?"

No. They were my treasures. She couldn't have them.

But Felisa figured out how to take my dance outfits anyway. Just like when she was in *parbulito,* a kindergarten student, and she sneaked into Mague's second-grade picture.

Despite her *travesuras,* Felisa was everyone's favorite. She made it easier not to miss Amá.

Su mujer

Didn't stay too long this time. When she returned from Chicago our *golondrina mamá* seemed different. She came back pregnant and about to deliver another child.

Back in Tabasco, she finally had my father's firstborn son, Juan José Hijo, a junior who came almost eight years after me, and after having had Margarita, Felisa, and María de Jesús, who didn't live long enough to see our brother.

In her hometown and away from him, she came alive. My father's absence freed her from his violence. In Tabasco, she became herself again.

Filled with music, my mother was our morning lark. Spontaneously, she could launch into a song. She was light on her feet and bursting with happiness.

When he was around, that wasn't the case. She became another person. She lost her spark. He sucked the life out of her.

She withdrew in his presence. She became the maid, tended to his every need, and filled his every whim, tended to his every wish.

We all thrived when Juan was away. No one missed him.

We liked him better as a memory.

When he was away, we could almost love him.

This time Amá had a surprise for us. Father had finally given in. He would let my mother bring us to the United States.

Living in *los yunaitis: Sin papeles*

Our permanent crossing to *el norte* took place when I was almost twelve. When my mother returned to Tabasco to get Felisa and me, it was 1960. She had been living with our father, Mague, and little brothers—Juan, Ernesto, and Tomás—in Chicago. Felisa and I had yet to meet the two youngest boys.

When they came to pick us up, Mague had changed; she was quieter. The only time she talked was to show off her English. To Felisa and me, who spoke only Spanish, her speech sounded like dogs barking. Anytime she tried to impress us with her *inglés,* we responded in the Spanish language of dogs: "Guau, guau, guau."

We made fun of Mague because we envied her. She had lived with our mother without us.

Still, we didn't want to leave our *tías.* Felisa and I didn't want to go with our mother.

We wanted to stay in the comfort of Tabasco. We liked living under the care of our great-aunts. With them we had everything, even if it meant putting up with Pepe's constant teasing.

He called me *pinacate,* the name of a round, black beetle bug that clicked like me with my love for talking. Because of an almost single brow that joined at her nose bridge, he called Felisa *cejas de burro,* donkey eyebrows. This *apodo* made her shave those eyebrows to put a stop to the nickname. Only got her a new one: *la calabera,* skullhead.

Pepe, who read Russian books, was a staunch critic of the *gringos.* Every chance he had, Pepe told me he saw no need for us to go to the United

States. The way he saw it, the United States had nothing over México. As the almost big brother that he became, he didn't want us to leave his mother. But he loved us, too.

In his bantering Pepe teased that the immigration would force me to deny who I was. That they would make me reject my country—force me to step on the Mexican flag.

"Josefina. No te vayas a los Estados Unidos. Cuando llegues a la frontera, te harán rechazar tu país, y te harán pisotear el estandarte nacional."

I cried, imagining myself spitting and stomping on the flag.

Didn't want to leave my little pueblo.

"They'll turn you into a *gringa*. Te harás pocha y nunca más volverás."

I cried because I wanted the option to come back, even though I didn't know what a *pocha* was. Didn't want to turn white. Didn't want to go.

But we didn't leave right away. Before going to *el norte*, my mother stayed about six months to have our papers fixed. Amá and I went to the U.S. Consulate in Guadalajara to see about visas to come to *los estados unidos*.

I remember going with her because that was when I saw the first black man in my life. He was a huge man, getting off the bus at the *central camionera*. Having lived in Chicago, my mother was accustomed to seeing blacks. She didn't pay him any mind. But she scolded me for staring, turned my head in a different direction, and told me I was being *mal educada*. She had not raised me to stare at people.

At the INS the *gringo* said to my mother, "You *necesitar* $1,500 *por muchacha*." He told Amá she needed to post a bond for each family member. Couldn't even imagine what $1,500 was like, much less double that for Felisa and me—we had lived on only $12.50 a month that my parents sent to Tía Herme for our care. That was a lot of money! I even imagined that they could have bought a car or a house instead.

When my father found out it would cost $3,000 to bring us legally into the United States, pressured by our mother's desperation to unite our family, he decided to do it *sin documentos*—illegally. Later, Felisa and I realized that this would be another excuse to take advantage. Still, we had no clue.

Soon we were packing our belongings and saying our good-byes.

We visited friends, teachers, and relatives. When we finished visiting all of them, we stayed inside the house, hardly wanting to go out as the time to depart drew nearer. Felisa and I cried for anything and everything—we didn't want to leave our *tías* behind.

The day came for us to leave—I was just a child.

My aunts disappeared into the mountains of Tabasco as our father drove away. With eyes clouded by tears and the distance, I was left with only that memory to cherish. I wondered if I would ever see them again.

Leaving Tabasco was like a funeral when no one dies.

My sister and I had no choice. We had to go to the United States with our parents.

The trip north took about three days and nights. We slept in the car, buying food as we drove.

On our way we crossed several Mexican states.

My father drove through Zacatecas. For the first time we were able to see a land carpeted by cacti. With its tropical and lush environment, Jalisco looked like a paradise in a South Pacific painting without the ocean. In Colima we ate our first seafood tacos. That was before my stomach *se agringó* and I had become accustomed to U.S. food. I don't remember Sinaloa. Baja California was a rocky desert. It looked like another world to me. Scantily clad in greens, the cacti of the desert jutted out to create a landscape that was unfamiliar. Red, brown, and golden colors, as well as rocks the size of boulders made the northern Mexican desert surreal. The tale of a white horse making his way to the border, "El caballo blanco" by José Alfredo Jiménez, played over and over again on the car radio. We finally reached the México-U.S. border.

Our father left us in Tijuana.

We stayed there for a while until he made arrangements for us to go across.

In Tijuana I met a distant cousin named Lupe who was about fifteen. She was pretty fast company. Tried to teach me to smoke Kools, "para mirarme más cool." Almost coughed my lungs out, vowing never to smoke a cigarette again.

I was easily impressed by my urban cousin, who looked city-slick with her makeup. She talked me into trimming my eyelashes because she convinced me that they grew longer when you cut and brushed them with olive oil.

I'll never forget Lupe. I still have a bald spot on my left upper eyelid by which to remember her. Deep inside, I wanted to look like Lupe.

She was so beautiful. I was so *rancho* next to her.

When my father finally came to pick us up, we crossed the U.S. border in his two-tone red-and-white Ford sedan. We didn't have to show any papers.

No one made me dance on the Mexican flag. I was asleep until we reached Los Angeles.

Migrations

Our first stop was either Watsonville or Aromas, near the Salinas Valley south of San Francisco. I remember the trees dripping with green and red apples and never-ending parcels of strawberry fields covering the ground. Big trees I had never seen before—fruit, eucalyptus, large oaks, madrone, and others that looked similar but were not—dressed up the land in deep greens, reds, and rich amber colors I had never even imagined. The mountains, as round as scoops of ice cream, were a deeper green than the ones in Tabasco.

I saw what I thought was a town, like a million fireflies all bunched up together in different parts of the mountainside. It looked like the Emerald City that Dorothy and Toto saw on their way home.

"¿Qué ciudad es esa?"

I was greeted with mockery and laughter.

"Josefina, ¡no seas pendeja! Es una fábrica de cemento. It's a cement factory, you fool," my father scolded.

We finally ended up in the fields of California after our long trip. Our family stayed with the Marquezes, and our parents worked the apple orchards. I don't remember how long we stayed. But I didn't like it, and no one could make me.

The best part of all this was meeting Richie Valens's sisters, who lived in Aromas and worked the fields alongside us.

"My brother is Richie Valens, the famous rock and roll star. I'm not lying! He really is our brother."

So what? It was no big deal to us.

"Tomás Méndez is my *tío*."

Claiming our distant relative who wrote legendary *rancheras* like "Cucurucucú Paloma" and "Paloma Negra," songs of love and romance that everyone knew by heart, we tried to outdo them.

Not wanting to be *arrimados*, we stayed only long enough to make the money we needed to get to the next place. It was then that Mague and I were drafted into the fields. Lost our appetite for apples or any of the fruits we picked. We hated the scent of the ripe fruit that clung to our clothes and turned our stomach. Felt as if we had been drenched in cheap perfume all day long.

We didn't have drinking water, and we had to hold our bladder or go behind the bushes in view of the other workers. Never had breaks, forced to keep up an adult pace. Tin buckets we carried cut into our fingers and blistered them until we grew calluses on our palms. Didn't take us too long to learn this wasn't something we wanted to do the rest of our lives.

After Aromas our next stop was Cupertino, California, *el rancho de los Mardesich. Las peras, las* cherries, and other farmwork awaited us.

"There is always work for those who want it," my father said in consolation, pretending that life wasn't as hard as it was. The gold-paved land he had imagined had not been kind to him. In the *gringo* world he had become just another pair of Mexican arms. It was the only thing he had: his work.

Up until then we had not gone to school. My father's fear of *las autoridades* kept us out.

There my sisters and I made friends with Sylvia, or Syl, as she liked to be called.

She was visiting her aunt and uncle, Tomás and Linda Raygoza.

A Mexican who thought she was a *gringa*, every chance she had Syl bragged that her relatives worked in the canneries, claiming that they were too good for the fields. She didn't even think twice about putting us down for working there.

A fourteen-year-old city girl, Syl introduced my sisters and me to rock and roll and the music of Paul Anka. We started to learn English with "Put Your Head on My Shoulder, tell me that you love me, baby . . ." which we knew as "Tu cabeza en mi hombro / dime que me quieres, baby . . ." because Mexican heartthrob Enrique Guzmán sang it, too. He was our Mexican wannabe Elvis Presley.

Syl tried her best to make us look like her, turn us into *gringas*.

She sneaked us into her uncle's house to see *American Bandstand* because she knew we had been ordered by our father not to watch it. He didn't want us to be perverted or become American-crazy with ideas.

Because of Syl, I finally learned who Richie Valens was; he was a Mexican with the last name of Valenzuela who sang rock and roll.

Our friendship was brief, however. Syl returned home to Tijuana before she had a chance to really turn us into *güeras*.

As the king of the house, my father finally decided to enroll us in school. He didn't want any legal troubles. My father had control of everything and everyone. Did what he wanted. But it was Tomás Raygoza, Syl's uncle, who pressured him. He saw how hard our father worked us. I think Tomás felt sorry for us. I heard him tell my father many times that if he didn't enroll us in school he would have legal problems: "Chepo, te vas a meter en problemas legales. Lleva a las muchachas a la escuela."

He finally listened.

We started school for the first time in Cupertino, California, thanks to Tomás.

School was not like the one I knew in Tabasco.

Didn't know English. Couldn't understand. I had no friends. It was lonely and hard. White kids made fun of us and excluded us. My sisters and I were the only Mexicans in school who couldn't speak English and probably the only Mexicans besides the two Raygoza children.

But home was what we knew. At home we played, climbed trees, and ran around with each other and the younger kids.

One day I climbed the fig tree that was two stories high in front of my house. Figs were my favorite fruit in the United States. They didn't grow in Tabasco. I loved figs. After eating all the ones on the lower limbs, I climbed the tree as high as I could to reach for more. Didn't realize how brittle the limbs became as they got smaller; however, I was a good climber and was up to the challenge.

"Ándale, ándale, qué buena. Traíme más," Felisa egged me on, clapping as I reached the top.

Fell down.

Passed out.

Felisa told me that Mague came to my rescue. They thought I was dead.

"Mague carried you upstairs. Two flights without complaining."

My mother and Comadre Linda brought me back with smelling salts. Amá looked worried, but she didn't scold me.

I broke my wrist, too. But my father ordered that no one take me to the doctor, just to teach me a lesson. Wasn't worth the expense.

"Chingada muchacha. Pa' que aprenda, ¡se va a quedar asi!"

A chirriona who climbed trees. Because I was a fucking girl who had to learn, my wrist had to mend on its own. It cost money we didn't have.

My mother and Comadre rigged up a splint. A crooked wrist bone is what I have to remind me of that day, and it still hurts with the cold.

Hated figs, even in photographs.

One good thing happened, though. An adult finally questioned my father's heartlessness in front of all to hear.

"¿Cómo que la van a dejar así? ¿Qué no tiene corazón mi compadre?"

It was all worth it to see my father squirm. ¡Me valio el chingazo!

Despite him, I found the joy in life. With other children around to play, we could almost feel human.

Limones in the Fields: *Jugando migra*

We used to play a hide-and-go-seek game we called *migra*. We thought it was funny that everyone scampered when the green wagons from the INS arrived.

I was too young to be afraid of *la migra*. But I did see many *redadas*, roundups of field workers, with grownups running every which way to escape. It was unfair that the INS came to arrest our *compatriotas* in their lime green *limones*.

Like *resorteras*, the slingshots we used for target practice, the workers jetted out from their rows. Didn't know how they found out *la migra* was coming. We didn't understand why they came to take them. Our friends and neighbors weren't hurting anyone. They were just hardworking people who became old before their time from hard work and exposure to the sun. They just wanted to make an honest day's living.

Don Lencho, wrinkled like the grapes that were left on the vines to dry, would often talk to us about *la migra*. From him we learned how workers felt about those raids, as he worried out loud about "having to figure out who will lend me money to come back, having to find another *coyote*, and having to stay to harvest my land in México."

The slowest of the bunch at forty-one years, Don Lencho was usually caught first. When they nabbed him, he tried to maintain his dignity— running and yelling in whatever language came to him.

"No seen in work, workeen ees no craim. No es pecado trabajar."

Don Lencho wasn't afraid, but he didn't want to get caught. He saw the INS as a nuisance, compared them to a toothache that doesn't go away or flies that keep coming back after you shoo them away.

Cursing at them at the top of his lungs as they dragged him into the paddy wagon *limón*—*hechando vigas*, spewing *maldiciones*—he defended his right to be here, his stolen land.

"Pinches huevones. Bueyes. Pa' trabajar sirvieran."

Called them a bunch of lazy *bueyes*, good-for-nothing oxen. Told them they should be big enough to work. Get a real job.

"Sonavabiches, yu don no har work . . . *sueltenme* . . . Le me go, *cabrones*."

La migra must have gotten a kick out of catching him. The only response he received from the agents was their laughter as they pushed and shoved him into the wagon.

But sometimes Don Lencho was given what he wanted—a free ride home.

"Vivo en Tijuana. Mandenme a Tijuana. Jom ees Tiajuana. Sen me tu Tiajuana," he told them in the best English that he could, hoping to improve his chances of being understood in his *inglés mocho*. It paid off. Don Lencho ended up in Guadalajara near his beloved Zacatecas.

Everyone was always on the lookout.

As the sun came out, so did the *migra* in the fields. The hide-and-seek would start over again. Pedro jumped fences; Juan hid under the abandoned jalopies; and Luisa found cover in the toolshed to escape the agents.

Scared me. Made me cheer for the ones who escaped.

Serapio, Cleto, and Teofilo weren't so lucky; they were caught. We knew their stay was temporary, unlike our *pocho* neighbors who lived without fear, even though we'd hear about them being sent back, too, by mistake! Sometimes they called the *migra* on us. Said we took their jobs— they could have mine anytime.

Mexicanos lost everything when they were sent back. Couldn't even collect the wages they had earned. *Más fregados*, having borrowed money to come across, they were sent home penniless. They went home with nothing—*ni un centavo*. Wives were happy to have them home but sorry that they failed to return with money. Adventures turned sour were something no one talked about openly. Soon, with the help of the wife and family, the cycle would start all over again. They sold what they had of value, borrowed money from relatives on both sides, and went to loan sharks to gather money for their return trip.

Don Lencho was best at this game. He could always borrow enough to return. It was almost as if he never left.

Still, the workers kept their hope. They knew they would return, and most did.

Back in less than two weeks, some found themselves working for the same bosses. Except for the debt they acquired, it was as if they had been here all along.

Spared in the raids, most parents were happy to have the day over with and ignored our _migra_ game. "It wasn't funny," some of the parents scolded.

"The _migra_ takes food out of kids' mouths."

"Families _en el otro lado_ don't have _dolares_ to support themselves."

"They stay hungry on the other side."

Some liked our language and the way we used the opportunity to learn English. How enterprising and smart we were.

When we started the game, we prearranged to pick the slowest kid in our group as _el agente_—it was always a boy, because we never saw women agents. We started the game by counting to two hundred. We decided on this number because it was what the workers paid to come to _el norte_.

It was no big deal to count that far. Most of us, even the five-year-olds, could count to two hundred; some could even count to one thousand. We counted so fast that two hundred felt like twenty. We had learned to count when our parents complained about the $20 it took to pay the gas and light, when we saw how many _tortillas_ it took to feed a large family of eight, and when we counted the licks our parents gave us when we got in trouble. One thousand was harder; we learned its value when Tomás bought his _canaria_, a beautiful yellow and black convertible car that cost him almost $4,000.

"Cientonoventaiocho. Cientonoventainueve. ¡Dooosciiiieentooooooooos!"

The slow-pokey agent screamed as loud as he could to announce his raid. We always knew that the slowest and most _sonso_ of the bunch would give us the best game. Kiki, _el suato_, took his job seriously; therefore, we often picked him. He played the part as if his life depended on it.

Ahí viene la migraaaa.

Ahí viene la migraaaa.

Ahí viene la migraaa.

Three times was the warning call. The chase began.

Hiding, we tried not to make a sound. Breathing low and slow so as not to give ourselves away, we became part of the scenery. Some kids hid behind the shed. Others climbed to the highest branches of the fruit trees. Some went inside parked cars.

The game lasted well into the evening.

Scaredy-cats gave themselves away every time. Didn't know how to be quiet or be by themselves. *El agente* was there to nab them, and the interrogation began.

"Paydro?"

"Haysoos!"

"Paanshow?"

"Hey, komo yamartay?"

"Day donday ser too?"

"Donday estar toos papeles?"

"Mai naim eees Plu-tar-co," chimed the boy we called Pluto because he could always get a laugh with that. The inside joke was that we all thought the name was strange and funny. That's why he said his name.

"Juat?"

"Juat eees yur naim?" *el agente* asked in his best English.

Not so *sonso* after all. His English did the trick. Smoked us out rolling in laughter from our hiding places.

We hated to get caught. Busted, we would have to sit out the rest of the game, staying in detention until we earned our way free. Then the game would start all over again. We played it every chance we had, creating a *teatro* for all to enjoy. We had the best time of all.

Making fun of the English of the INS agents taught us not to fear *la migra*. Also, my parents were here legally and had no fear of being sent back. Good thing they didn't teach us to fear them. Guess it helped that they never went after us either and that our parents didn't tell us we were here illegally—we acted and felt as if we belonged.

When we moved out of the fields into city life, things soon changed. We didn't have the freedom of our games.

Get Out if You Can: In *Sal ¡si puedes!*

"We're moving," my father announced. He liked keeping us off balance, didn't even let us know where we were moving.

With every move, we took only our clothes. No furniture. No appliances. No dishes. We had only each other.

Each move could have been a beginning for us. But for the change of place, we were captive under the watchful eye of our father the jailer, whose mistreatment became more intense with every move. No one knew us.

Sleeping on the floor had become routine. We didn't care if we had a bed or not; whatever space we had, we had to share anyway. What I feared most was the loneliness and isolation. I became morose and shy. Every move made it that much more difficult to make friends. As it was, our movement was restricted to the house, with our only escape being the walk to and from school, if we were registered to attend.

When I was about twelve, we moved once again. This time we went to the city.

In Sal Si Puedes, a barrio of east San José, my father rented a two-bedroom duplex for our family of eight. It was during that move that we went to the *segunda* and bought used furniture. We started with two noisy metal spring beds and two bunk beds for the boys. It wasn't our father who bought them. It must've been Amá. In her thrifty way, she figured out how to do it. We even got a black-and-white TV. Still, we were not safe.

The girls were given the room with no doors that was on the way to the bathroom. We all shared the space. Our bedroom was an open U. It was the area between our parents' and brothers' room. Have you ever seen a railroad house? It was like that. But the girls' room had no doors. Unlike the three boys, who each had their own bed, a door, and two parents to protect them, we were exposed.

We girls had only two beds, and we had to share them. With no windows and only a small closet, we also got a secondhand, musty old chest of drawers. When we put our clothes away, they reeked of mothballs. We had nothing on the walls, maybe a *santo* or a calendar with the Sacred Heart, but there were no teen idols like Fabian or Elvis. Pukey green, our room was a prison.

The house was quiet because it was at the dead end of Summer Street. Our home wasn't cold or hot.

Most people who lived nearby were immigrants or poor. Our neighbors were from Texas. Spanish and English were spoken in our neighborhood, but the scoldings around the neighborhood were in Spanish. Living behind wafer-thin walls, we could hear the "talking-tos" outside. We received ours inside.

"Ya es hora. Vengan. Metanse." It's time to stop playing and come inside.

"Yaaaaaaa."

Most people who lived in Sal Si Puedes were good people. Never heard a cuss word outside, but I heard them all from my father's mouth. *Chingada pa' aca* and *chingada pa' alla* was all we heard, and more often than not the words came with blows. He didn't discriminate among the women in his family; he targeted us girls and my mother equally. Only his boys were spared.

Besides the murmur of daily conversation, once in a while we heard the neighbors fight and raise their voices. But it was rare.

We didn't get to really know the neighbors. We weren't allowed to step outside without permission. Not wanting to get beat by our father, my sisters and I seldom violated that rule. Moving to the city didn't really make a difference for us. We were still cloistered in the madness of his castle. This move spared us only from the farmwork. I suspected he'd always figure ways to make us pay for our keep.

The Nightmare Begins

Without a bed, I became the migrant bed sharer. Just had to figure out with which sister I would sleep. That took work because I had to be on the lookout for my father. Had to figure out what he was up to.

In Sal Si Puedes, I caught on to his tricks. Didn't know when, late evening or early morning—I didn't know. Our bedroom was on the way to the bathroom without doors to keep him out. Everybody was asleep. I didn't hear him. I just knew it was my father.

That night I may have slept with Felisa. I was on the edge of her mattress, having instructed her to sleep close to the wall. She was about seven, and I was about twelve. Because I grew up with Felisa and felt especially close to her, I loved her enough to put myself in her place.

I wore cut-off jeans as pajamas. They fit really tight and were really hard to put on and pull down. For added protection I slept in jeans with a zipper or maybe jeans that buttoned up. Having long learned to read my father and his moods in order to fend him off, I guessed his target right. He found me instead of Felisa when he reached out to touch between her legs. It must have been hot; I don't remember his removing the blankets. That's when I caught on to his tricks. It wasn't the first time someone had tried to touch me down there. My cousin Ramón had tried and failed. My screams had scared him away.

However, this time the scream did not come easily. Gagging from the panic, I tried to yell. Only an "argh" escaped my lips.

Froze. Pretended to be asleep.

Realizing what was happening, I kicked and tried to scare him. Couldn't yell. The screams that could reach my mother's ears wouldn't come out.

Knowing he hadn't reached his target, he cussed at me. He was pissed when he found me fully dressed and realized I wasn't Felisa. He whispered hate-filled *maldiciones*, cursing loud enough to scare me, but not so loud as to give himself away.

"Pinche, jodida muchacha. ¿Qué te crees? ¡Ya verás!"

In those hate-filled Spanish words he loved to toss around, Juan accused me of thinking myself too big, warning me that I would pay for it. That was wrong. I couldn't obey him with that. It was wrong and it felt dirty. I wouldn't put up with it.

He left in a huff. My screams finally came out.

Amaaaá. Amaaaaaaaaaaaá. Amaaaaaaaaaaaaaá.

Why didn't she see what he was doing? Couldn't she tell by the way he leered at us? I saw it. It was those looks that helped me guess who would be next.

"¿Que tienes, Josefina?"

Wanted to know what was wrong. Amá came and hugged me to let me know she was there. Comforted me.

I went silent and told her nothing. I didn't want to lose my mother.

Having lost her once, I didn't want to lose her again, although I loved living with Tía Herme.

I was afraid of losing my family.

I loved her, and I knew she wanted to be with him. Couldn't understand why she would want him, though.

Kept the silence.

In Tabasco, when this type of thing happened, no one went to jail or was even prosecuted, even though the whole town knew about it. I had to take care of it myself. I didn't think my mother could do more than comfort me. I had to take care of my sisters. They had me to stop him.

How weird. How sad!

I finally figured out why we had so few friends and why we were kept inside the circle he created. It wasn't to keep us out of harm's way but to keep us to himself. What a sick mind. What an evil man I had for a father!

Sheltered and dressed in clothes that hid our bodies, we were conserved for the god our father—the creator of victims for himself.

Seen but Not Heard

Ruled by our father, our social life depended on him. He ordered us to stay out of sight and to refrain from speaking until we were addressed. Unless their children came with them, which was not too often, he kept us away from his visitors. There were times I wondered if they thought my father would hurt their children. If this was ever the case, I was never able to find out.

We were restricted to the backyard. He controlled our movement and appearance. No pants or shorts allowed. *Como aleluyas*, as we called the Holy Rollers, we were made to wear plain, frumpy, old-lady dresses, old maid colors, and long skirts with buttoned-up blouses that had to cover every part of our body.

Only *putas* dressed differently.

Metidas. Always inside the house.

En la casa. Siempre metidas.

We were always inside the house.

He reigned over the radio and the stations we chose. The black-and-white TV was there only for his enjoyment.

Once, when we dared to risk watching *American Bandstand*, our brothers told on us. We were whipped for having dared to violate the TV rule. For turning us in, our brothers were allowed to see cartoons and *The Three Stooges*. To punish us, he sent us away when he was watching *Bonanza* and *Lawrence Welk*. Although it was the only thing we could see, I was happy. Who wanted to see old people dancing, anyway? Didn't care about seeing stupid cowboys making fun of the Chinese cook. It was only by accident that we got to see the Beatles. He was watching *The Ed Sullivan Show* the night they first appeared in the United States.

But he didn't control my reading. I loved to read. Many a night my mother came to remind me to turn off the hand lamp I used to read under the covers.

The good life escaped us. Our father's dream became our nightmare. The United States offered very little for us. We lived like captives in our own home and had no one but ourselves. But we soon found comfort in school again.

School was a safe place to be. I created friendships behind his back. Friends from school could never come over, and I never went to their homes.

Sometimes my sisters and I stayed after school, regardless of the consequences. Backed each other up. Knew what to expect. What we were given was the belt, a telephone wire, a tongue lashing, and a dose of humiliation in front of all to see. The larger the audience, the more brutal he became. However, we were willing to accept that for the moments of freedom we stole.

Like cattle taken to pasture, our routine was predictable—home and school and home again. The only thing that changed was the route we took to get there, so long as we arrived on time. How sad! My sisters and I weren't allowed to think. Couldn't stray from his plan, whatever it was. No school activities, academic or otherwise, permitted.

Chattel.

Property.

Black and red ruled our lives.

We lived inside the black of fear and wallowed in the red of anger, bleeding inside. He was a master at hitting, and we were his punching bags. He hit us, beat us, and cussed us out on a whim, made us feel worthless. Beat my mother in the privacy of their room. We could only imagine what it was like by her groans, her muffled screams, and the moans we heard. Made it scary not to see. Never saw any marks on her. Never sent her to the hospital.

I did see him beat her one time. It was the day he tried to take Mague with him to the store. Mother stopped him. She told him he would not take her and pulled Mague from him, to protect her. He turned into a caged animal that had been pent up too long.

Reacting to her efforts to protect Mague, he threw my mother around the living room for daring to talk back to him, for daring to stand up for my sister.

Her head hit the wall with a thud, sounding like a rubber tire against the floor. She stood. Her lip was trickling with a thin thread of blood. Angrier, and with enough force to make her body bounce, my father pushed her against the couch. She tried to protect herself, but her force was nothing against his brute shoves and pushes that bullied her into submission in front of us. She deserved it for standing up to him. She wasn't supposed to talk back. Couldn't talk. She and her girls were to be invisible and mute. She had learned to eat the anger—kept it inside. I hated him, but Mother was too afraid to kick him out.

All of us lived thinking we imagined the violence. Shelved much of it aside. Told each other it wasn't that bad, that others had it worse. We plodded on, pretending it no longer hurt.

Except for our school life, we were the walking dead. I often wished I had the heart of a Medina or a Huerta then; I wouldn't have been afraid to kill him.

Muertos y matones

Because of the violence in my life, I would often contemplate how life must have been for my aunts in Amá's village, Rancho de Cosalima. I often dreamed of being one of their children, so I could do away with him.

In Mexico we had our Hatfields and McCoys. Only they were called the Huertas and Medinas. The memory of their feud and the violence my *tías* witnessed helped me to see that my life was not as bad. I was alive.

It all began with male relatives born of my two aunts who married into enemy families—*primos hermanos*. The way it was told, depending on who tells the story, it was the Huertas or Medinas or the Medinas or the Huertas. No one can really remember how it started. Someone killed someone else, and that's when the "somebody-kills-someone, someone-kills-somebody-else" cycle began. It was not uncommon for us to hear that a Medina had been shot again and that a Huerta was soon shot after the Medina died. Both of my aunts lost their sons to this family feud. Officials kept a blind eye to the goings-on. Saw it as a *pleito de familia*. No one ever got caught or punished for the crimes.

We held multiple *velorios*—six or eight. I lost count. *Sangre de su sangre*, blood of their blood—every time we buried one of the killers, *uno de los matones*, I wondered how my aunts dealt with so much hatred.

Then there was the death of Santos Medina, who was my aunts' relative and uncle to cousins who killed each other. He was skinned alive. Castrated. His body was dumped in the river to rot. Because I was a five-year-old girl, his death gave me nightmares, prepared me for the horrors I would confront later. Nothing could have been as bad as what my *tías* saw.

The wake for Santos Medina was at our house. His procession began from our doorstep. I was never more frightened by a *muerto*. However, Santos did not join the *espantos y fantasmas* said to roam our home. He never came to haunt us.

He shouldn't have died. He wasn't part of their silly feud. He was innocent.

When I thought about Santos, I'd often wish my father had been in his place. Santos was a generous and kind man. He had never hurt anyone. My father loved to hurt others. Why is he alive? *¿Porqué siempre se quedan los malos?* Only the evil ones live.

The Huerta and Medina feud ended with their migration to the United States, but our violence was just beginning. While stories of *muertos* and *matones* haunted me, there were ghost stories that made me appreciate life.

<hr>

Ghosts and Goblins

We played games. Told stories about *la llorona, el diablo y los espantos*. A flawless *mentirosa*, thirteen-year-old Chela was the best storyteller in Tabasco, next to her mother Chayo.

Chela was the best prankster. *Esa Chela, ¡volanda pica!*

We called her *la abeja* because, like a bee, she stings on the run. And, to boot, she didn't even die! Her *chistes* were so *pesados* that there were times we wished her dead. But we didn't really mean it!

Hanging out with Chela meant trouble. The last prank she pulled was the final night we spent in Tabasco before leaving for the United States. Chela and her mother had come to say good-bye all the way from their homestead of Rancho de Cosalima, my mother's hometown.

That night my sisters and I were in bed. Exhausted. Waiting for the next day.

Chela, faking sleep, was up to something. So we tried to stay awake. She was too quiet. *Nos olía mal su silencio.*

Suspecting she was up to something, we tried to stay awake. Couldn't do it. Must have dozed off.

As in a dream we sensed something in the room. Too scared and stupefied by the ghost stories she had told us that night, we had tried to stay awake. Didn't help.

Suddenly, without a sound, a shadow draped in something appeared in the silvery light.

Mague was the first to scream. "¡Ay, Amá, Amáaaaaaa! Un bulto," an apparition's frozen hand had touched the soles of her feet!

I saw the shadow crawling about, too.

My sisters claim I screamed, but I was too big for that stuff. Didn't cry. Didn't let those little things bother me. There were more important things about which to scream.

The cold-handed figure dancing in the moonlight continued to touch all our feet in delight. It stopped only when Felisa screamed. Must have been the apparition's soft spot for babies.

"¡Ayyyyyy!¡Ayyyyy! Mamá. Un espaaantooooo. ¡Veeengaaa!"

They say I was the loudest of the bunch. But they lie.

Felt like an eternity before Amá came. She must have left to get the kerosene lamp because we had no electricity. Probably had difficulty finding it in the dark.

Amá appeared, lamp in hand. Came in to find Chela rolling on the floor with laughter.

Chela confessed how she hit on the idea.

"Couldn't sleep. Went outside. Noticed a bucket of water on the side. I decided to put my hands inside it. To see how cold they could get. Wanted to touch your little feet like the ghost your mother claimed to have felt. To get my fingers to feel like icy bones caressing the bottom of your feet! Give my cousins something to remember me by."

¡Qué risa nos dimos, cuando nos rímos!

What a laugh we had, after we got over being scared!

She gave us a memory we still talk about. *Chela, la abeja,* stung again. She had a good teacher in her mother, Chayo.

Tía Chayo

She was the perfect storyteller. Even had special effects, like her black and white shawl—a *rebozo* with specks like the ones we've seen in the *godorniz's* eggs—and a black widow dress that enveloped her like a cocoon. Swaying back and forth, her hair flew like the witches she described.

Fue el día que se le apareció el diablo a tu abuelo. It was the day the devil appeared to your grandpa.

I could imagine my grandfather face-to-face with *el chamuco,* the charred one. Made me cuddle up to whoever was next to me. Turned my skin into a turkey that had just been plucked.

"Your *abuelito* went to a dance without our mother's permission."

Chayo told her stories with whispers, pauses, and the tilt of her head, as if to warn us in which direction to take caution.

To get there, he had to travel at least three hours by horse. He usually had a pleasant ride, enjoying the sounds of the birds and the occasional interruption of silence with the swishing of leaves and the trotting of the horse.

My father had no trouble getting to whatever local dance was going on, despite the religious warning of perdition from his parents. He loved dancing so much that if it were up to him he would dance all the time.

One evening, not having the blessing of his parents to go dancing, Papá Apolonio decided to sneak out when everybody had gone to bed. The three-hour ride was filled with unexpected surprises. The clanging of horse-drawn carriages that were nowhere in sight and the smell of rotten eggs scared Papá Apolonio; he had no idea from where all this was coming. The air reeked of sulfur and burnt lumber, but nothing was on fire. This seemed strange to him; he knew the road very well. There was nothing around that could give that foul smell. Thinking this was his imagination or that he was going crazy, but more concerned about getting to the dance, he continued trotting at a steady pace. Then the horse he was riding suddenly stopped and almost threw him. But Papá Apolonio was able to calm the stallion and continued his ride.

He couldn't wait to get to the dance.

A local *banda*, in those days they were made up of drummers and buglers and a tag-along guitarist or two, played.

He had the time of his life.

You'd think he would have learned his lesson.

I guess *el cuernudo* must've been in a generous mood that night. For the horned one decided to spare Papá Apolonio.

His return home was trouble-free. There were no noises. There were no disturbances. The smells were gone.

Moved by his love for dancing and against his better judgment, Papá Apolonio decided to try his luck at the *baile* one more time.

Ésta vez, no le fue tan bién que digamos. This time around, he wasn't so lucky.

Halfway into town the strange things that had happened before began to appear. This time, however, the horse he rode threw him off and disappeared into the night. Considering this but a minor inconvenience, Papá Apolonio decided to walk the rest of the way. He thought he could stay with relatives and spend the night in town. He didn't worry about the horse; it would find its way home as it had other times.

He must have walked about a quarter of a mile when the stench of sulfur gagged Papá Apolonio. He could hardly breathe.

Suddenly, he spied the figure of a man to his right. He rubbed his eyes.

When he looked, there was nothing there. He turned to the left. Nothing. Unglued by the fear, he quickened his pace.

"¡Apolonio!"

He heard his name called in a voice that sounded as if it came from deep inside a cave. It didn't sound like anyone he had ever heard. Papá Apolonio ran and tripped. As he was getting up, a man-like figure stood above him.

"Mire, ¿qué hace por aquí? ¿Qué? ¿No aprendió su lección la semana pasada?"

Satan asked why he hadn't learned his lesson.

"¿Quién es usted?" stuttering, a terrified Apolonio asked. "What do you want from me?"

The devil responded, "Tú me conoces muy bién. Ya sabes quién soy. Ven conmigo. Ahí no te faltará la música y ¡podrás bailar noche y día! Ja. Ja. Ja. Ja." Chayo repeated the story in a broken English she had learned in the United States to get by as the wife of a *bracero*. Repeating the devil's words, she made her story more expressive: "Ju no me bery wel. Ju no hu I am. Kom wiz me. Ju wuld lak for noting. Yul haf music to danz dai an nite. Ja. Ja. Ja. Ja."

Chayo danced, acted, and played each of the parts as if to make them more alive.

Don't play dumb, the devil continued. You know who I am. Come with me. You won't lack anything where I come from—you'll dance day and night.

He tried to tempt him with beautiful orchestra music playing in the background.

Very confused and extremely frightened, Papá Apolonio asked what he wanted from him: "¿Qué quiere de mí?"

An earth-shaking laughter came from Lucifer's core. *Ha. Ha. Ha. Ha. Ha. Ha. Ha. Ha.*

Papá Apolonio didn't wait for a response. Instead, he sped away from the eerie figure. No one had to tell him; he had just confronted *el chamuco*. He had seen his feet—one was the hoof of a goat, and the other looked like the claw of a chicken.

Papá Apolonio still cringes when he recalls the day the devil wanted to take him—*cuando el chamuco . . . ¡el diablo se lo quería llevar!*

Praying for his life all the way home, Papá Apolonio made it in record time. To this day they say he will not dance.

"This must have been a great sacrifice. Los Méndez have always been known as exceptional dancers," Chayo said, ending her story.

The voices and the sounds made by Tía Chayo, *la cuentera*, were enough to make us behave. That was the price.

We feared sleeping by ourselves. Frightened out of our wits after hearing about *el demonio* and *la llorona*, the weeping woman who killed her children, we were perfectly behaved for stretches at a time.

These stories taught us to understand and to live with fear—to know that it does not take anything away but that it gives. Also, made the adults proud of our comportment. People were heard to comment how well behaved the Méndez children were and encouraged their kids to be like us.

Chayo later followed her children to *el norte*. *Sin papeles. Sin trabajo. ¡Sin nada!* Without papers, without work, and without fear she quickly found herself with more than enough to do. Chayo cleaned houses. Chayo took care of children. Chayo picked up cans and bottles and recycled them for cash.

Before long Chayo earned enough money to buy herself a home in Tabasco.

Even though she was my father's sister, she was good.

Chayo now works to give her paycheck to the church.

There are times I still feel the loss for not having had the opportunity to know relatives on my father's side. However, with our migrations they became specks of memory in our minds.

❧ *Abuelos y difuntos*

The only grandparent I barely knew was Abuelo Apolonio, my father's father, because I was too young to know the others before they died. One day long ago when I was but a tot, Abuelo came to defend my mother's good name, to have a talk with our father, to set him right about the way he should treat his wife.

Relatives and townsfolk admired him or mocked him. Abuelo lived on the outskirts of Tabasco.

In his waning days people talked about the time he traded two cows for a couple of mules. Who would do that? Especially when he was losing his land and his wealth and the *rancho* was about to be sold. The cows were going to a family with nothing more than a small lot and many hungry mouths to feed.

Amá told me that Abuela Cuca was Apolonio's love and that he did all he could to give her the best life. They were married almost forty years before Abuelo lost her to cancer. Mother and Abuelo were the ones to take care of her when she became ill. They always seemed to be gone to the big city and capital of Aguascalientes, for her care. Don't know how they got there. No one had cars, and the roads were not easy to travel. Must have used his horses to get her there or relied on those rich friends who brought cars from the United States to take her. He stayed with her. Brought her back and forth until there was no hope.

During her illness, she lived in our master bedroom until she died. Don't remember much about Abuela other than her frequent need for water. Asked me to take her some when no one was there to do it. Soft whimpering and moans were all I heard before she died. Never complained. Abuelo was at her side, leaving all things for others to tend to. He lost much of his wealth to take care of her.

The only memory I have of her is a black-and-white picture. She must have looked like my father, but I could never see him in her. She was generous and gentle. He was her opposite.

Amá kept us from her. Wanted to protect us from the memory of her wasting away into nothing.

When she died, *mujeres* in black dresses were the first to arrive at her wake. They showed up in large numbers. Not all of them knew our *muertita*. I suspected some were there just for the food and the music. Rosary beads in hand, with *mantillas* or *rebozos* covering their faces, the *rezadoras'* prayers sounded like buzzing *zancudos* to me. Like an amplified *llorona* wailing, their sounds increased in intensity as the time to march to the cemetery drew closer. The *barullo* was enough to wake her, to let our *muertita* know we loved her.

After her burial, kin and strangers returned to share stories about Abuela. Made her seem like a saint or legend. Her human frailties and sins were forgiven with death.

As I was saying, when Abuelo came to set my father right, I don't know how I got away with it, but I saw everything that happened.

It was in the patio near the big pomegranate in plain view for all to see. I couldn't hear what Abuelo was saying, but I could see my father was *agitado* with Abuelo. My father bowed his head. Not even a peep came from his lips.

Couldn't believe it. I wasn't used to seeing him that way.

Abuelo commanded attention. He knew just how to get it.

Father appeared to be listening.

Then the talking stopped.

Grandfather pointed to the pomegranate. Sent my father to cut a small branch. Took it to Abuelo. It was long and thick like the *riatas* the ranchers used to guide the horses. It made me break into a sweat. I knew what *baritas* were for—we called them discipline twigs.

"¡Ínquese!"

Heard Abuelo ask my father to kneel in reverence to his authority. Creeping ever so quietly, I drew nearer because I wanted to hear more. Now he had it coming.

"No merece a esa mujer que es tan buena con usted. No quiero oir que maltrata a su mujer. Las mujeres no son para maltratarse. Merecen nuestro respeto y amor."

For the first time in my life, I was learning about the importance of love and respect. That my father was hit was not the point. Grandpa had come to teach my father to honor and respect his woman—the chosen one in his life. Abuelo could not tolerate that he was mistreating our mother. In the language of dignity and honor, he spoke to him like a real man, using *usted*, which is really like "thou." Came to remind him that he was not raised that way. Women were to be taken care of and treasured. They were to be loved.

That's why he came. Abuelo didn't want my father to hit or abuse my mother. Abuelo warned him that if it happened again, my father would have to contend with him.

Then Father knelt in the middle of the patio. And Abuelo started hitting him.

The swishes from the twigs on the branch sounded like the leather bristles Abuelo used to guide his *burros* and *caballos*. On my father's skin the twigs sounded like the crackling of pork rinds when Chenda poured her chile on them to make *cueritos en chile verde*.

Abuelo was a man of respect, a man of his word. He had fourteen children from Abuela and his second wife, Belén.

Although he was poor later in life, he never lacked for food, as he reaped the rewards of his generosity and respect. Could always borrow a horse or a mule to harvest his land. Never expected anything from anyone, even his children. Didn't ask them for anything.

Abuela Cuca was not the only one to die in my home in Tabasco. A year later, when I was five, my little sister María de Jesús died from encephalitis before she was three months old—she became an *angelita* only because Amá baptized her before she died. Didn't want to condemn her to a life of limbo, not yet having earned the right to go to hell. Didn't have time to sin. Not contaminated by him—my father made her but never met her—she was spared.

Nuestros muertitos gave me life. Wanted to have them around to pretend they would protect me.

If only my *abuelos* were here, I could have used their protection. Wouldn't have been alone. Abuelo could have used the twig on my father. Made him stop.

Maybe my little sister María de Jesús was lucky. Death saved her from my father. That's probably why scary stories became our diversions from the terror with which we lived.

Espantos y tesoros

"Amá, tell me about the time you got scared," we girls would ask, requesting that she share the legend of the buried treasure and the ghosts that haunted our house.

"Ay, ustedes y sus espantos. You and your ghost stories," Amá responded somewhat annoyed, but knowing how much we liked them, she began her story. "Pero, bueno, there were many things that scared me. *Una vez* someone pulled my feet. Petrified me. Another time I heard a clay pot break into pieces under the bed. I don't know why, but I thought someone was underneath. Thinking something was there, I looked below. I found nothing. Didn't want to call for help. It was just you girls and me. Like a scared child I pulled the covers over my head. Only thing I could do was pray to the Sacred Heart and go to sleep."

As little children in Tabasco, we were always looking for treasures. We wanted to find the shimmering lights that led to the pot of gold. But what for? We had all we needed. Sometimes we dug deep enough. It was then that we found a few coins here and there, but they were not old or gold—just *centavos* someone threw to give us kids a charge. Kept us entertained and out of the way.

Legend had it that a treasure was buried where the earth glitters of gold. We heard this story many times. In one of Chayo's many tales, she told us about some *vecinos* who went digging for gold. They found the shimmering. They set up and started to dig, dug well into the night. Then the greed of the *compañeros* took hold, *los agarró*. Instead of finding a treasure, they found bones. All that work for nothing—there was no gold, just some old bones. Sometimes Chayo made it more dramatic by telling us that one of the *compas* was pulled into the hole by skeleton fingers. With that fantastic tale, how could we believe in treasures?

In our Tabasco house many people saw that light emanating from the earthen floor of my mother's bedroom. I guess no one believed there was any reason to dig, or we just didn't want to find any bones.

But our neighbors the Fraustos believed. My *tías* claimed that the Fraustos kept an eye on my mother's bedroom and that they always showed interest in it after we left. Everyone knew that *revolucionarios y cristeros* had passed through our town during those wars of the early 1900s and they buried their loot.

Our home had been in the family for generations, and it was said that there were treasures buried there. Many around town repeated stories about the looting of grains, food, and money.

"Se llevaron el dinero."

"Robaron el granario."

"Nos quitaron la comida."

"We had to tend to them so they wouldn't take advantage of us. That must've been what got them to choose our house. They took our money, turned our house inside out, and ate all the food we had. To boot, we had to attend to their every whim so they wouldn't take liberties with us."

"They used our house as headquarters. Those shameless soldiers took over the home of *el bisabuelo*, Sixto. To protect us, he didn't help or stop them," Chenda recalled. She told me that her father's only concern was for his daughters. The thought that the soldiers would take them as *soldaderas* to service some *pelado* kept him alert.

Depending on who came to town, *los oficiales* favored the Méndez property. It was near the center of town.

"It could be the *federales*. Another time it could be the *cristeros*. Didn't have to agree with them. Didn't have to support them, so long as no one got in the way," Chenda sighed.

The Fraustos always had questions about our home. They asked us if we ever found money. Wanted to know if we ever dug up any coins. What a bunch of *preguntones! ¿Qué les importaba?* We thought they were too nosy.

Still, they managed to have us talk about the light in my mother's room. Though no one except Mother had actually seen it, people over the generations had heard about it. We talked about it all the time, as if it were a fact. I began to believe I had seen it myself.

Our *tías* later wrote my mother to tell her that the wall on the Frausto side of the house had fallen. Someone had dug holes into her bedroom. Without being told, we imagined it was the Fraustos. The holes were where my mother heard the sound of the pot breaking, underneath her bed, where she saw the light shine. This is the very spot where they dug out the pot of gold. No one saw them. But shortly after the wall was found in ruins, the Fraustos, who had no money, moved to Guadalajara because they bought a business and a new house. *¡Qué suerte!* How else could they have done it?

Unlike some in Tabasco who had relatives in the United States or people with money, the Fraustos were poor—they must've found the treasure. But we'll never know for sure.

Our family house is now in ruins. It sits there for my mother to some-day reclaim, but most important, it sits to honor her as a Méndez. Abuelo left it to her as a testament to her sacrifices, instead of willing it to his *desobligado*, good-for-nothing son. But, along with the fantastic memories, that home concealed many horror stories, too.

❧ Living in Fear

"¿Eres de este mundo o eres del otro?"

When he walked by my room, my heart beat out of control. I rushed back from school with jaws clenched in fear that I would not make his curfew. The only time he would leave me alone was when I did my homework or buried myself in my books. Always had to watch him for clues. When eating our dinner, he had to be served first; we were served after his boys. Eating only what we were fed, we weren't allowed to ask for seconds.

To deal with my fear of him, I whistled a tune or prayed some Hail Marys inside my head. But he wouldn't go away.

I could not ask if he was from this or the netherworld because he was real and vicious.

Soon after we came here, he violated me; however, I wasn't his intended victim. That night I slept with Mague. She had taken the inside of the bed against the wall. What happened was scarier than anything I had heard or seen so far.

Didn't know we had a *mañaso* for a father. What a pig!

I soon lived the horror stories I had only heard or read about. On top of my underwear, he rubbed me. What was scariest was that his touch brought good sensations that confused me. Gave me a stomachache. Made me want to throw up. Didn't know just what to do. Tossed and turned, making a big ruckus that scared him away.

Must have figured out it was I instead of Mague. Scared the *chamuco* away.

I wanted to get away, but I had no place to go. I was trapped, and the devil himself was my captor. Living with him was like riding the rickety roller coaster, swimming in the river with moccasins, and not knowing what was up or what was down. For us there was no difference between day and night, except for school, which kept us sane and out of his reach.

Life was as he saw and called it. We were supposed to act on his demands, do as he said, live with his choices—and shut up about it.

If all else failed, a song always helped to quiet the fear. "El himno nacional," the national anthem, came in handy.

> *Mexicanos, al grito de guerra*
> *El acero aprestad y el brindón*
> *Y retiemble en sus centros la tierra*
> *Al sonoro rugir del cañón.**

* Mexicans, at the cry of battle / Prepare your swords and bridle / And let the earth tremble at its center / At the booming roar of the cannon.

It was almost a call to war. If only I had an army behind me. Sometimes other songs would do. Belting out the *cucurrucucus* of my father's own uncle, Tomás Méndez, became a call to safety. *¡Cucurrucucú! ¡Cucurrucucú! ¡Cucurrucucú!*

Whatever song it was, I learned that it took only about twenty words to be in the comfort of sleep. *En los brazos de Morfeo,* the Greek god of sleep, I could pretend nothing was bothering me.

I was living with a monster, and he knew he was king. Didn't have to say it, he just acted the part.

Buscando abrigo y no

lo encontraran

Searching for shelter

they will never find

El rey del machismo

José Alfredo Jimenez's song blared on the radio during our visit to the Marquezes, our relatives in Watsonville. I cried when I heard that song. My father was the song.

> With money and without money
> I do what I damn well please
> And my word is the law
> I have no throne and no queen
> And no one to understand me
> *Pero sigo siendo el rey.**

Papá, a word I refused to use because of his cruelty, really believed he was king and that our home was his castle. He thought of himself as the owner of his wife and his daughters, to do with what he wanted. Every chance he had, he pushed his weight around, reminding us who held the reins and that his word was the law.

"Estas chingadas viejas tan solo sirven para parir hijas. Damned hags, only good for birthing girls. I don't lack any doubts that Alejandrina will have another *chingadas muchacha*," my father complained when Amá was pregnant with her fifth daughter, my sister Sonia.

I tried to plug my ears. *Estupideces. Estupideces.*

My mother hates that word, but if there was ever a time to use it, it was now. But I knew better. So I stayed silent, eating my feelings.

"Let me tell you, Compa, yo tan solo quiero niños. Only want boys. What the hell are girls good for, anyway?" said my father to Compadre Pedro as they discussed Mother's pregnancy during our visit to Watsonville.

Even though we were forbidden to eavesdrop on adult conversations, I

* But I continue being king.

could no longer ignore his comments. *Pinches estupideces.* Damned stupidities!

Boldly, I decided to correct him.

"Son los hombres que hacen las hijas," I said with all my sixth-grade knowledge. Men are the ones who make girls . . . *Son los hombres que . . .*

My face made a sound like the clay *piñata* that cracks with the thud of the broomstick from the force of his backhand. And I was his clay *piñata.*

My head jerked. My jaw made a sound like a walnut when it's hammered open.

I wanted the earth to open up and swallow me whole. Become invisible.

He shamed me in front of all to see. But I didn't feel in the wrong; he had just humiliated me. The fear or embarrassment made everyone go silent.

Anger welled up in my neck, giving me the strength to gather my dignity. I rushed out crying, not because I was wrong but from the humiliation of it all. Everyone, including our hosts and my mother, felt mortified by his tantrum because they felt it was a private affair. They wanted nothing to do with it. My mother had been long silenced with his violence. No one ever mentioned the incident. It was as if it never happened.

Fear is no excuse for silence. They should have said or done something.

Our meal was ready. We were called to eat.

At the table everyone acted as if everything was fine. No one said a word.

Despite the cracking of my jaw, I tried to eat, but I couldn't. Wasn't even able to open my mouth from the stress of the blow. The rest ate in silence as I watched.

The smells of garlic and lemon, the marinade of the *carne asada*, and the *fideo* gave me hunger pangs. Even the scent of roasted *tomatillos* and toasted *chiles de árbol* weren't enough to open up my jaw.

The stabbing pain stopped me from eating. Couldn't chew.

He won this round and I got my serving.

Con dinero o sin dinero—when it came to us—he even ruled outside his home and controlled our mind.

Chapas: Inside Latches

I had buried that memory in the string of forgotten abuses from him. Had erased it until Felisa reminded me that I put latches inside our bedroom doors to keep our father away. It was around 1961 when we first moved to Santa Clara from Sal Si Puedes in east San José. I was just twelve.

My sisters and I finally had a room—it had two doors. One led to the bathroom we all shared. The other faced the kitchen hallway.

That damned beast could finally be contained. We could now control our own space.

I don't recall where I found the latches.

With Felisa's prodding, it all came back. It was while my father was at work one day. I remember proudly installing them. I used an old-fashioned metal iron to pound in the nails and a kitchen knife to put the screws in place. When I finished, I felt satisfied that we would now be protected.

The satisfaction didn't last long, though. When he arrived home from work that day and discovered what I had done, he turned into a madman. He took it out on our mother, making sure we witnessed the beating. He was using the drama to intensify our fear of him and put us in our place. What right did we have?

"Chingadas viejas. Esta es mi casa. Aquí soy el rey y se hace lo que yo diga."

"*Vieja*, tell your fucking daughter to take off the latches. Now! Fucking hags. This is my house. I am king, and in this house you only do what I tell you to do," he directed his words at my mother as he spewed venom our way.

"Pina," calling me by our family nickname, Amá asked me to remove the latches. The tears bathed her face, and her voice cracked as she told me, knowing she had no choice but to obey him.

He didn't wait for me to remove the safety latches. He beat me unconscious. But I don't recall that part.

Felisa told me "it was with a belt." I must've repressed it.

I guess I didn't need to remember that. It wasn't out of the ordinary for him to beat me. I grew used to it. I don't ever recall a kiss or a hug from him, but I'll never forget the burden of his beatings. My body and mind are roadmaps of his madness. He was a trickster, just like those depraved *mañosos* I had heard about before.

≈≈ The Bathroom

The bathroom was his alibi. That's where he spied on us.

It was in Santa Clara, the bathroom was between our parents' bedroom and our room. Our sleeping quarters were conveniently located, as if he had planned it that way. Doors, and even my mother's presence in the next room, did little to deter him. He always found a way.

The bathroom was his door to betrayal. Where he peeked at our bodies.

There were times after he had gone to the bathroom that Amá came to check on us. Found us dressed. Satisfied, she would return to bed, having made an effort to protect us. Because his violations were limited to touch, she never found evidence. We said nothing.

Our mother did not consciously support his abuses. She was deathly afraid of him. He controlled even her mind. But inside her own head, she must have suspected something. Too afraid to let herself imagine, she let him control her thoughts.

When he sneaked into our bedroom at night, he came through the adjoining door. If I had guessed his target right, he would find me. When he reached me, because I was labeled a crazy sleeper I would freely and with good aim kick him and scream as if I were having a nightmare. Usually scared him away. Sometimes I hit my target.

As a last resort, with *miona* as a nickname, it was not beneath me to urinate in bed. This usually kept him away from me. It stopped him for that night. But I received a great *monda*—his word for beating—for no reason at all. Soon, I became as cunning as he, outfoxing him at almost every turn.

Heavy Sleeper

"¡Te apachurra un tren y no sientes nada!"

Describing me as a heavy sleeper when I was young, Amá would often comment that a train could run me over and that I would not awaken. Finding that funny, I just laughed. I had no fear of a train running over me; there were none in Tabasco.

That was when I had no fear of intrusion. That was before my father violated me.

But I learned to cope. Leaving my body or learning to sleep through his touch was preferable to the realization of his abuses. This initially worked for me.

After that I could wake up at the drop of a straight pin. Even a sigh from him would launch me to my feet.

Pretending it wasn't me when it happened, I imagined it was someone else. Pretending I wasn't there, I often left my body. Pretending it didn't happen, my mind went blank. Then, pretending no longer worked.

My sleep patterns changed when I stopped his abuse. All it took was saying, "No! Don't *you* touch me again!"

To my surprise, he stopped. But he continued molesting my sisters.

I tried to warn them, without spelling it out. Didn't want them to continue experiencing the pain and the betrayal. But they were not even able to listen.

When I no longer feared his clawy, flaming hands that burned me inside, I learned to be a light sleeper to protect my sisters.

I became their alarm, jumping at the smallest noises. Easily awoke to the buzz of a fly.

Mother didn't notice my sleep patterns changing. Wherever we moved, I was always the first one to wake up. That wasn't all that changed; he kept us off balance moving from one place to the next.

Santa Clara

As with all migrant families, we didn't remain long in any locality. After San José, Santa Clara became the home to which we returned. The harvest or my father's fear of being exposed kept us moving.

When we moved there, Santa Clara was an old town with old houses. There were only a few Mexicans, mostly Portuguese, Italians, and a few more Filipinos. We arrived at the peak of anti-Mexican sentiment, when speaking Spanish was not permitted in schools, even when you could speak no other language.

Landmarks in our neighborhood included the canneries across the train tracks, such as Van de Kamps. Neto Sausage Company made us feel at home again with its Portuguese sausage good enough to pass for the Mexican *chorizo* we longed to eat; it stood around the corner on our way to our elementary school. Santa Clara University was a short three to four blocks away, depending on how we got there. Seven blocks away was Saint Clare Catholic Church, where my brothers made their Holy Communion and where we attended mass with our mother and never with our father.

IDES Portuguese Hall was around the corner, close to the park where my brothers would often escape to play. The Portages, what we called them in those days, had their Holy Spirit celebrations in this hall, with marches down the streets of the city led by queens and princesses of different ages dressed in their finest white lace gowns. They wore their shimmering rhinestone tiaras, each leading different sections of the march along the route.

We talked to no one. No one talked to us.

When I entered Fremont Elementary, Mr. Sánchez took the time to introduce me to my classmates. He spoke Spanish and encouraged those who spoke it to break the collective agreement of silence, encouraging them to speak to me in the language of their parents.

This had not happened previously. At the other schools I had become part of the furnishings. They put up with my presence or ignored me.

"This is Josephine," he said kindly as he encouraged them to "help her make new friends." He added, "You speak Spanish and know those who do. Help her be comfortable in our school."

"I don't speak Spanish," Berta Gomes answered.

"I'm Portuguese," said Tiki Soares.

As Mexicans, we felt ashamed and remained speechless when interacting in the public world of the community. The tensions we experienced from speaking a language that was not valued became so confusing to us as Mexicans that we even found ourselves feeling uncomfortable speaking Spanish. Just about made us lose our voice, too.

When we rode in our family car, as our father listened to KLOK, our regional Spanish-language station's sound of *música ranchera*, we'd often slink down on the seat. We wanted to hide from view, so as not to be identified with the music that blared. Shame turned us into the original lowriders.

Waiting in line at the Mexican movies, we wanted to become invisible, so as not to be seen until we entered the dark safety of the theater. There, we blended into a world that was ours, where the Spanish language dominated. Inside the familiarity of the Liberty Theater, conversation among the moviegoers became a welcome relief instead of a burden. We could deal with the annoyance of crying children and even the smell of *pedos*, farts, feeling safe among our *gente*, even if they were strangers.

Ostracized by the silence in the schools, we continued speaking Spanish at home until we learned the language of the *gringo* community. There was no choice. I soon learned English.

Speaking another language, however, did not free us from his clutches. He continued creating new ways to trap my sisters and evade me.

Love of Learning

I was no longer his victim, so he figured out other ways to get to me. As he could no longer molest me—a young thirteen-year-old daughter who still played with dolls—he found other ways to make me miserable.

I ignored him or figured out ways to get back at him, until he picked on school. He knew I loved it. Tried to make me drop out more than once, but I resisted.

When I was almost sixteen and in the tenth grade, I overheard him tell my mother that he wanted to pull me out of school.

"No! No! No! Not school!"

It was the one place I could learn. It was the only place where I could be normal, where I was a human being. It was the one place I was rewarded for thinking and knowing.

I had heard enough. Wouldn't put up with it!

Desperate, I went to him and told him what I overheard. He laughed. He knew he was finally getting to me.

Without fear of his retributions, I challenged him. "Before you take me out of school, llamo a la policía. En este país es contra la ley no ir a la escuela. Si me saca, lo meterán a la carcel."

Grabbing books stacked on my bedroom shelf that he knew I had read, I threw myself at his mercy. "In this country, you can be put in jail for not sending me to school," I repeated in English, hoping to touch whatever shred of humanity he had.

In a weird way I think my father enjoyed the confrontation.

Outwardly, he appeared not to care, but I think he enjoyed the challenge. I was as daring as he, but for a better cause. I wanted a better life, and all seemed to think that education was the way to many things. So did I.

He must have been in a good mood that day. Or perhaps I threw him off guard with my gumption.

I don't know why he spared me. He didn't hit me. He didn't take me out of school.

The issue was never raised again, and I remained in school. Committed myself to my learning and my reading.

Hoe-Say-Feena—Hosie Who?

My name has a bicultural and bilingual history. One began when I was born; the other when I came to the United States. This was never made clearer than when I entered school.

Names are important. They matter.

Names link you to families and record the day of your birth, except when the name on the calendar is Ignacia or Zenaida. These would have been the names my sisters Mague and Felisa would have received. However, with my two sisters our parents ended the tradition. They, unlike me, were not given their saint's name, the name on the calendar for the day of their birth—they got their own.

Good thing our parents named my second sister Margarita, we soon learned. Calling her Nacha—an endearment intended for Ignacia—was the losing side of a fight with her, who on our father's insistence was named Margarita because of a *Norteño* song that was in style when she was born. She could have had Ignacia as her name; instead, she lucked out.

> *Margarita, Margarita*
> *No me subas tan arriba*
> *Que las cosas en el árbol*
> *No duran toda la vida.**

---

* Margarita, Margarita / Don't lift me up so high / That things hanging on a tree / Don't last for a lifetime.

It's not a very significant song. The story, rather than being about Margarita, is about a suitor who claims not to want adulation as he seeks it.

Knowing she was named after a song, we often searched for songs to tease her. Our favorite one was "La mujer de Don Simón."

> *Señora Margarita*
> *Mujer de Don Simón*
> *Le gustan los tamales*
> *Y las tripas de ratón.**

A silly song about a woman who likes *tamales* and rat guts was no fun. Singing it to Mague and calling her Nacha guaranteed us a fight. Nacha was also a nickname for *nalga*, butt. She didn't like being called a butt.

As I said, Felisa also was not named after the saint of her day. Instead, she was named after the nurse who took care of Abuela Cuca when she had surgery for cancer in Aguascalientes.

Don't know why most of my siblings and I had only one name, unlike the rest of our friends, who were María this and Guadalupe that or something or other. Even boys were called José Marias, whom we called Chemas, or José Guadalupes, also called Lupes; they had the middle names we coveted.

When I learned that I could get a confirmation name to add to Josefina, I began practicing combinations. María Josefina. Josefina Guadalupe. Josefina María. Guadalupe Josefina. Chayo Josefina. Each combination made my name much more *mexicano*. It rang of celebrity to me.

Convinced I needed a second name to go with my only name, I discussed my options with friends and relatives. After much discussion I decided on Xochitl Josefina, a name I borrowed from one of my cousins; Xochitl meant flower in Nahuatl, the Aztec language.

"Indian names are stupid," Prima Choco, short for Socorro, said when I told her of my choice. "Use Flor." She advised that Josefina Flor or Flor Josefina sounded better because it was a good Christian name.

* Mrs. Margarita / Wife of Don Simón / Likes to eat tamales / And guts of *ratón* [mouse].

Having decided on a name, I couldn't wait for confirmation day to arrive.

It finally came.

The bishop brought an air of celebration to the *pueblo* like no other parish priest ever had, having come from the state capital of Zacatecas. His arrival gave meaning to the saying *Cada venida de Obispo*. Bishops rarely came to our town and only made themselves visible during major ceremonial occasions.

On the long-awaited day of my confirmation, all I received was a slap on the face to teach me humility. That slap sealed the fact that I would forever remain *Josefina a secas*—just Josefina.

Names carry histories and memories. They're living stories to tell.

In the United States, in sixth grade, students and teachers asked my name. In response I sounded it in Spanish syllables. "Jo-se-fi-na. Mai naim ees Jo-se-fi-na," I repeated, hoping to squelch the giggles that came with the "Hosie who and Hosie what" of my classmates.

Trying to speak English, however it came out, was not easy. I couldn't understand their laughter. I couldn't figure out why their tongues tripped over my name.

It was simple. A fine name for a nice Catholic girl born on St. Joseph's day, my patron saint, and for my father's middle name of José.

I liked it. The only problem I had was that I had no other one to go along with it. It was just Josefina—*Josefina a secas*.

My name was not changed until the INS (the immigration agency) anglicized it to suit the English tongue. With more power than the bishop, in the living room of our house the agent changed my name with the stroke of a pen when he translated it on the spot on that temporary immigration form he completed for us to stay.

"Your name is Josephine. That's what we call your name in English," he said as he wrote it on the permit that he gave our mother to make us legal. Had he asked me for a middle name, I would have given him one. I would have claimed Xochitl. But he didn't. Even in English I remained just Josephine.

Josefina became my family name. Josephine is my legal and public name.

Friends and family soon learned to call me Josie, except for my mother, who to this day still calls me "Yosi." Still, I will forever be *Josefina a secas*.

Whatever they called me, it would always be better than the names my father used when he talked to me, and definitely better than he treated us.

The Blanket Game

After the nightmare in Sal Si Puedes, he must have sensed I had the potential to tell. I was not chosen to play the blanket game anymore, unless I volunteered. To protect my sisters, I often found myself enlisting in his game, especially when my mother was present.

Armed with a blanket to cover himself and his victim, my father picked his prey. Tried to ignore me, as I kept my eye on him.

In his sick mind he thought he was giving us a treat. He made it look as if he were picking mates for a team, calling on one of my two sisters to serve as his pillow.

He would place his head on my sister's lap, cover himself, and, in the presence of whoever happened to be there, he would masturbate her special place. Must've gotten a kick out of having a secret audience.

My stomach turned just to think about it. Having been part of his game, I knew what he was planning to do.

I don't remember where Mother was. I guess she was too busy with her brood—stair steps: Juan, Ernesto, Tomás, and Sonia. And, I think, my baby sister in the belly.

She must have been there, but I can't recall exactly where.

Can't remember the color of the couch. Don't remember the designs on the wallpaper, only the vertical lines. It felt like a cell.

The only thing I can picture is the fireplace in the living room; it was in the farthest corner of the room.

Everything was gray, without life. It felt like a rainy day, and I was always crying inside.

I had no hope. I prayed just to survive. Still hoped for a miracle.

With butterflies in my stomach, there were times when I volunteered to be his pillow, just to protect my sisters. I sought my mother out, wanted her to know I was the pillow. Hoped she would hear me when I protested and stopped his play. I had planned to outsmart him. And I did.

I didn't let him cover me. Pushed the blanket and his paws away from me.

"Yo no tengo frio. ¡No me cubra!"

I would loudly protest, refusing the shield for his sin, claiming not to be cold as I refused the blanket. He could not insist, for if he did he would have exposed himself to Amá. Once again, I had outfoxed him by giving her a heads up.

I knew I would pay for my daring, however. Sooner or later, I knew I would pay for having challenged his authority. The first chance he had, he would make sure of that.

"Josefina. Bring a belt! Traime un cinto."

"Yo no hice nada. I didn't do anything."

We both knew the beating was the price for having volunteered in the game. His sadistic whipping made me feel victorious anyway because he had not touched my sisters. I won. I protected them for the day.

"¡Chingadas viejas! ¡No sirven pa' nada!"

It wasn't enough that he beat me, he had to demean me by cussing me out and telling me I was a good-for-nothing fucking hag. Glad to be one, if it meant I could stop him.

As God had not come to our help, someone had to be there to protect us.

Doubts and Blasphemies

Church became another foreign world when we came to the United States. *La madre iglesia,* as we had learned to call it, became another institution in which we did not fit. We had only one Mother Church. We had left her in México.

Mass was still in Latin. But at the new church, no one looked like us.

They didn't pray for us. They didn't pray with us. They didn't pray like us.

They had other *santos y vírgenes*. They didn't have the ones we had learned to rely on to mediate our troubles and pain. La Virgen de Guadalupe was gone from our lives. An Irish or Italian saint, I forget which, replaced Santo Niño de Atocha. Portuguese icons substituted for la Virgen de San Juan de los Lagos. All we had was a statue of a white woman clothed in a white dress. Instead of the expected red, white, and green of our Lupita, the Virgin Mary wore a blue cape the color of the sky. A light pink and blond angel, rather than the Indian who held up our Tonantzin, hoisted her. How could we pray to such a virgin? We didn't know her. She could not provide us comfort.

Out of habit we continued to attend church. We religiously went to Sunday mass. Didn't go to confession, though. Lacking language skills, we could no longer eavesdrop on the moral purging of others, as we had in Tabasco. Church was no longer a magnet. We couldn't even confess our sins, even those that were perpetrated on us. What was the difference? English. Latin. All of it was English to us.

No one listened. No one heard our call for help.

Rather than going to keep track of those who practiced the Catholic faith, we became the facile target of the eyes of strangers—the Mexicans on display at the Italian, Irish, and Portuguese Catholic Church of Saint Clare.

There were so few of us. We really stood out! Church became something we did on Sunday, a meaningless act to get out of the house.

Feeling out of place, we began to make excuses about going to mass. Only our friends could drag us there—with them it was a social event.

Church in Tabasco had been more fun.

Dominus vo biscum. Sounded funny to us. Giggling, my sister and I would turn to each other, saying in Spanish "Your brother is cross-eyed." *Tu hermano es un visco.* This was as close as we could come to giving the Latin prayer meaning. The banter continued until we became lost in the ceremony of things.

Et cum spiritu tuo became "And your uncle, too." *Y tu tío también.*

Still hear those childhood voices when I've had the chance to go to a High Mass, and that has been infrequent, at best.

Our aunt could not understand our chatter. But this was our game, our way to make sense of the ritual. It kept us from being bored. And they let us be.

In Santa Clara *ora pro nobis* brought us to attention. We understood it as a call to prayer. We joined in prayer, hoping the language we tripped over was a direct line to God. *Ora pro nobis. Ora pro nobis. Ora pro nobis.*

We were good at the standing, kneeling, and sitting parts of it. We knew those by heart. What we could never learn was the meaning of the Latin we heard. Don't think the priests wanted us to anyway.

Father never went to church. It wasn't for men.

Church was the responsibility of mothers. And children had to attend.

People claimed that God really listens to children's prayers! Never really believed that, not having had any of mine answered.

In times of anger I told Mother that God didn't exist. "How could He, with the life we live?" I wondered why He had forsaken us.

"No, digas blasfemías. Te castigará Dios."

Cautioning me not to blaspheme, Mother warned that God would punish me, as she told me to stop doubting, questioning His plan and design for us. She didn't want me to suffer His wrath. But my questions continued, and her warnings became less forceful.

"Aren't we living a life in punishment already?"

"Be a good Catholic."

"Carry your cross."

"Don't disobey your parents."

"Honor your father and your mother."

Heard her warnings over and over again. Our parents and the Church controlled our lives and ignored us at the same time. Where were they when we needed them?

Ora pro nobis.

Dominus vo biscum.

Et cum spiritu tuo!

Aaaaaaaaaaameeeeeeeeeeeeeeen!

La regla: Santa señora del mes

In English or Spanish or in the Catholic world of mass, our lives continued. Couldn't stop the changes of growing up; I matured into a young woman in Santa Clara.

Mother never told us about menstruation, *la regla.* I never really talked about my period with her. Learned all about it in elementary school. Still, the delay of my period was the topic of conversation for my mother and her *comadres.*

"¿Todavía no empieza? Hasn't she started?"

"She's almost thirteen."

"Is something wrong with her. She's late, isn't she?"

I was glad not to be in my sister Mague's shoes. I had more important things to worry about, like repeating the sixth grade for the second time, after having missed two years of elementary school with the move to the United States and our father's refusal to enroll us. I wasn't worried about the delay. I was glad not to have one. Mague had started hers when she was barely eight.

Then it finally happened. I was playing on the monkey bars. Red rivers ran down my legs. *Manchas* as big as the sun marked my change into *señorita*hood. There were no warning signs. I had no pain. It just came.

Luckily, one of the playground teachers, a man *pa' acabarla de fregar,* heard the kids making fun of me. So he came to investigate.

Children were pointing at my skirt spots and laughing. It wasn't bad enough that I was almost thirteen, and in sixth grade, and playing on the monkey bars. Now it would be hard to be a *chirriona* with the freedom of an eleven-year-old.

When the teacher looked at me, I could see pity in his eyes. Using his sweater, he covered me and took me to the nurse's office, as if he had done it so many times before.

The nurse professionally said, "Oh. You started your period," not really looking at the *manchas* on my skirt. I felt silly.

"Dearie, this is your mother's job."

She could have at least given me a *garra* to put on or something to wear from the lost-and-found closet that she kept. But no, she was too cool to deal with me. Instead, she dismissed me to the school counselor, who took me home.

When we arrived, my mother invited the counselor to come inside, offering her something to drink. Then Amá said, "Ay, look! Hurry up, go shower. Change your clothes," in a Spanish that was interrupted by the counselor, who was letting Amá know she had to go back to work.

"No, Mrs. Méndez. I have to go back to work. Your daughter can stay home for the rest of the week."

Good thing my father was gone. Otherwise he would have seen the mess through his peephole in the bathroom floor.

I really didn't want a break from school. But a whole week! Four days off for starting my period?

"It's not as if it were Easter week or Fourth of July," I mumbled. But maybe it was best; I could stay home and watch the monster's moves.

Don Chepo, el desalmado:
His Lordship Mr. Chepo, the Soulless One

Everyone loved my father—family, friends, and acquaintances. All who knew him claimed he was a very good-looking man with a generous heart. He knew just how to endear himself to others. But he was menacing to his family while being giving and generous to others, even strangers.

They called my father *Don* because of his ways with others, although he lacked the pedigree or social status of the name. Don Chepo was the ultimate contradiction. In our private life he was the devil incarnate. In public he was "Good" itself. He was deceitfully good.

Of medium stature with a strong body and good physique, he was a fastidious dresser who liked to look his best whether wearing jeans or a three-piece suit. Jet black hair adorned his strong jaw. He had a fine Roman nose in which he took much pride and sensuous lips accentuated by two moles on the upper left side of his mouth. These beauty marks, two dark kisses, united him with Mague, who was born with the same marks on her face. In the same place, with the same shape, my sister and father were linked by those exclamation points emphasizing their beauty. Wearing a look of death, his eyes resembled those of a stuffed elk hanging in the trophy room of a hunter's lodge. Those eyes came alive only when he was out to harm someone, stunning those he hunted. There were times when I caught a glimpse of sadness and pain inside those eyes. But that was rare.

Over time our family sought reasons for my father's behavior and his treatment toward us. More often than not, relatives passively blamed his mother, as family members gave knee-jerk excuses.

"It must have been the horse-riding accident that Abuela had when she was seven months pregnant with Tío Chepo," offered one of his nieces.

"Pudo ser when Abuela fell off the horse that she was riding to Cosalima," chimed another.

"He was hurt when Abuela fell from the horse, and her legs were caught in the stirrups. She was dragged for miles." In her innocence, Mary attempted to cleanse the father she never had a chance to know, but I was glad she never knew him beyond the three months he was there. Thank God for that!

There are other explanations for how he was. Others claimed he was spoiled rotten, as the only brother in a family with four sisters: Rosario, Luisa, Estela, and Sára. Perceived as his surrogate mothers, they were blamed for coddling and spoiling him. Not surprisingly, they blamed the women again!

As with many macho stereotypes found in Mexican lore, Don Chepo loved to drink. With liquor in his belly, he thought himself invincible.

Under the influence he was demonic. He used alcohol as an excuse. When he was sober, he claimed not to remember what he had done when he drank. Heard from others that my father was cruel in the way that he did his women chasing. *Un viejero de primera*, he paraded women in front of the house for my mother to see the competition. Wanted to keep Amá in her place. Must've been *la Culebra*, but it could have been Rosa I saw. *En la putocracia del hombre, ¡mí padre fue el número uno!* There was no doubt in my mind. In the hierarchy of debauchery, my father was number one.

As to who my father was? There are partial truths in all of these explanations. Other reasons remain forever hidden. But the reasons are immaterial.

Era muy complicado y fanfarrón—a big showoff and not easy to predict, that's the way he was. People say he was a great horseman and a hard worker. He performed stunts in regional *charreadas*, the Mexican rodeos. As a *charro* he was fearless. One time he took his horse inside a *cantina* and kept it inside just to show he could have his way. Sometimes he even gave it tequila. If it was good enough for him, it was good enough for the horse. In the many stories my father told, he always played the lead.

Dropping out of school in the fourth grade, my father went to work the land with Abuelo Apolonio. It was theirs, after all. He had no choice but to be a hard worker. Don Chepo chose the life of a migrant worker, a field hand, when he could have worked his own *huerta*.

No one can explain why he would leave his own land to toil for the *gringos*. But that he did. There, his ways with people soon made him a foreman. Later, he found immigrant men to work the fields of South Texas, doing a contractor's job.

None of us ever had a *real* father in Don Chepo. However, he was the exceptional dancer who taught me *danzón y el paso doble*. He took great pride in having introduced the *chachachá* to Tabasco.

He could belt out a *ranchera* in the style of Miguel Acéves Mejía, preferring renditions of Tomás Méndez's *huapangos*, trying to outdo his famous uncle. On a lined notepad he would write verses to songs that played in his head. Claimed to be better than the best. The record player we had, off limits to us, stored 78s by Chopin, Beethoven, and Verdi.

Often found him sitting by the Victrola in the hallway, leaning his head on the console speakers as if to blend with the music. Could always hear the flaw in the songs.

Don Chepo, my father, was a man without a conscience who, like the Tin Man in Dorothy's life, had an empty space for a heart. But I don't know if my father ever wanted one. Still, I am barely beginning to understand him and the pain he carried.

His stories gave me a glimpse of the father he could have been.

Mi padre y mil moscas

If I close my eyes, I can still see my father lighting the bonfire to gather us for his *cuentos*. *La lumbre* was our call to join the circle. The bonfire announced his stories.

When he told his tales on his infrequent visits to Tabasco, kids and adults alike came from every corner of town. Even those children who had not gone to school because they were too sick found their way to the *lumbrada*.

The glowing and dancing flames lit up his handsome face. In a weird kind of way, he was almost beautiful.

Didn't look sinister. Didn't seem evil. He looked harmless.

His voice made him a fantastic figure, appearing bigger than life. When he told stories, he became a child.

Mil moscas was my favorite. Still remember how it started.

There was once a young boy named Cande. He was a hard worker, ambitious, and caring. Having lost his mother, father, and all relatives who tied him to his land, the only thing that kept Cande back were his deep roots.

One day a tiny island principality sent word that the royal couple was looking to rid their land of *moscas*. Flies had invaded their island.

They tried everything to get rid of them. Couldn't do it. Word of the problem reached Cande. He had heard that the princess, an only child, was deathly allergic to flies, and the king and queen were beside themselves. They had to get rid of the flies at whatever cost. They would have done anything to help their princess. Valuing her more than all the riches they had, the king and queen promised everything in exchange for a cure. *De pilón*, whoever cured the princess would get her hand in marriage.

The way they saw it, if the chosen one were able to get rid of the flies, he would merit their daughter. Acting in her best interest, they felt certain she would agree.

Cande looked into the problem. The more he studied it, the more he felt compelled to act.

Like nothing before, this problem lured him to leave home for the first time. There was nothing to hold him back.

Cande wasn't the only one. The royals' call for help received a tremendous response.

From places far and places near, people came and went. They tried many things. Nothing worked.

People tried everything they could. But the flies multiplied.

Many from faraway kingdoms continued to come with their magical cures—incense of all types, eucalyptus leaves, and other plants reputed to kill flies were burned, hoping that the smoke would drive them away. Some even concocted a frog powder, thinking it would repel them. This approach brought a few laughs from the islanders.

People continued to try everything they could.

Nothing worked.

The flies multiplied.

Finally, Cande enlisted the help of *la curandera* Domi. He believed in her. She had helped him many times before. When his parents were ill, she had prolonged their lives long past the time of their predicted demise. Domi had saved the day for him then; he believed that she could do it again.

Cande decided to place his trust in her.

After exhausting all the possibilities, the only solution she could find was to change Cande into a frog. As we all know, frogs are the flies' natural enemies.

Not thinking twice, nor limited by fear, Cande quickly agreed to the transformation. This was a challenge he was willing to take.

At his urging, Domi rushed to work up an incantation. Tails of frogs, eyes of toads, webs of duck, skins of snake, and other secret ingredients would do the trick. She had the recipe. It would not be the first time she had turned a human into an animal, but it would be the first frog she hexed.

"Beware. Do not pollute the volunteer's heart," the recipe cautioned.

If an impure heart were the driving force for his need to change, Cande would remain a frog forever. Yet there was a loophole: a kiss from the princess would give Cande his human form back, but a soiled heart would neutralize the power of that kiss.

His intentions were good. She knew he meant well.

In his heart Cande knew he was doing right. He felt he had made a difference in the world. Cande didn't fear living the rest of his life as a frog. He was satisfied knowing that he was doing all he could to help the princess.

Domi finally finished the potion. Still, before releasing it, she had to make sure Cande's intentions were pure.

Certain of his intentions, Domi gave Cande the potion in the teat of a cow's udder, instructing him to drink it in a secluded place. Otherwise, the magic would not work.

Soon after, with his potion tucked against his breast, Cande left for the faraway kingdom with his sack.

When he arrived, he went to the palace and sought an audience with the king and queen. He introduced himself as the holder of the secret weapon that would kill the flies. Having dealt with many charlatans, the royals impressed upon Cande that he would be beheaded if he failed.

Their threats didn't stop him.

Having proven that he was not another frog-by-night, Cande rushed to a secluded spot. He didn't want to waste any time.

Secure in his plan, he drank the potion.

It was a good thing Domi made a potion that left Cande's wisdom and *cariño* intact.

Shortly after ingesting the concoction, Cande appeared as a frog but with a he-man's appetite. He immediately went about exterminating the flies.

Slurp, slarp, slurp, day and night he combed every corner of the island, gulping every last fly he saw. *Slurp, slarp, slurp.* He didn't stop until they were all gone.

Good thing for his intelligence! Knowing that flies have eggs that hatch, Cande-as-a-frog cleaned every pool of water where mosquitoes are born. He inspected every lake and every river to stop the next generation. With his man-as-a-frog appetite, Cande drank all the filthy water he could.

It wasn't too long before the flies were eliminated. He had met the first challenge.

Because of his bravery and hard work, the princess now freely roamed the island, released from her imposed quarantine. The next challenge was to get the princess to kiss Cande, so he could return to his human form.

He wasn't worried. Cande was sure that everything would be all right.

The frog kiss turned out to be easier than expected.

The king was so grateful that when Cande-as-a-frog came to the table for the celebration, he saw Cande in the frog's eyes. He lifted the frog and kissed it on the spot. Without even thinking, the princess did the same. When her lips touched his frog skin, Cande turned into the noble peasant that he was.

It was love at first sight.

As decreed by the royals, Cande and the princess got married.

Not all was perfect, though.

Rumor had it that Cande's speech changed into a slurpy slang that was difficult to understand.

Others claimed his tongue remained that of a frog's, making it difficult for him to speak.

Whatever the case, this didn't stop the princess from knowing his heart.

Having rid the kingdom of flies, Cande became known as *mil moscas* forevermore. *En esos tiempos, mil* was infinity.

This is the one I remember best. However, our life with our father was neither a fantasy nor a fairy tale. *Mil moscas* is the only clue I have of his empathy and love. His wickedness was readily evident to me.

Juan the Peeping Tom

In the bathroom we all shared, there was a big hole between the commode and the tub. He had a makeshift bed in the space below, in the basement. From there he would spy on us.

I don't think his fantasy was to see us use the john. I think it was our nudity he relished. And the only way he could peep was in the darkness of his cave, where he would not be found out.

I didn't know this until Felisa told me she had busted him. One of the many *mañas* my little sister told me about, when she spoke about the day that she caught him peeping.

"I had just taken a shower. My back was itching, and I was afraid a spider had bitten me. I got on top of the toilet lid to see my back in the vanity mirror. No spider. But as I stepped down, I looked at the floor and saw that my father's dirty eyes filled the missing space between that crack in the wooden floor."

"Hadn't you ever noticed it before?"

"Had no clue it was there. Leering at me the way he looked at the

Marilyn Monroe calendar pictures that he kept in the basement, he made me feel like throwing up right then and there. But I couldn't react. Wish I could have poked his eyes out, but for a moment I was frozen in fear. The only thing I could think of was to stomp on those evil eyes. And I did. Then I ran away crying."

I was the only one she told. Didn't tell Mother. It would have upset her. She didn't need more surprises about her husband.

Determined to stop his peeping, Felisa made it her daily duty to cover the hole whenever we showered. This was one place he could not invade her. She would see to that.

Why would she tell me this? Didn't care to know more of his depravities.

Didn't she realize this was another thing that I could do nothing about? I was powerless and knew it. But she may have realized I was better at watching him.

Spoiling his fun, I kept him on the run. It was the only way I could survive.

Mague

My sisters were special. Mague was born right after me, and Felisa was fourth of nine. I wouldn't have traded my sisters for anything or anyone. But there were times I wished I were the only child.

Mague took all the best features of each of my parents; she was beautiful. She had a light tan complexion, a heart-shaped face, stunning lips, and full eyelashes. She looked like a delicate antique doll. She was built with fine features and had the constitution of someone made to weather the hardships of life.

From an early age Mague accepted her role as a girl. She, more readily than any of us, helped with the chores, took care of the children, and assisted Amá to attend to all of us.

Mague, my younger sister, didn't walk until she was about three years old, but she talked a lot. Her inability to do *solitos* and to walk was a concern to everyone in the family, but she was too young to care either way. To get around, she slid one cheek at a time, legs in front steering her like a three-wheeled bicycle turned upside down. Didn't need to crawl, she got by just fine.

"Estoy lista para caminar."

Ready to walk, she bull-horned for all to hear. She wanted to impress Abuelo, who was there on one of his few visits. *Como si nada, la chilpayata* Mague stood up and walked as if she were a diva on the stage wearing wobbly high heels.

"Le dije que yo podía andar," she said, looking at Abuelo as she strutted her brand-new steps.

She had warned, "I will walk when I'm ready and willing."

And sure enough, as she would later show us, Mague kept her promise.

Abuelo gleamed with pride for the child who decided when to walk. From that day forward, Mague became Abuelo's *favorita*. And she became an *andariega*, she who likes to walk and explore her world. With her fans, boys and girls alike, she would create havoc in many areas of the city.

I remember a fight she had with a fat and smelly boy named Tony who had her pinned down, in a dust-flaring, flipping and kicking rumble. She wouldn't give up. She kept coming back at him, throwing all her six years of life upon him. Finally, tripping him and getting under his belly, Mague flipped Tony. Though he won the fight, she grabbed a fistful of hair, managed a few scratches, and threw some bites in for good measure.

No one wanted to fight her after that. Walking away in anger, she yelled, "Cuando yo sea grande, yo también tendré una pajarita, ¡entonces me la pagarán!"

Somehow Mague understood that a penis gave them the upper hand. That's why she always said that when she grew up she would also grow a little penis, and then they would pay! *¡Mague no era rajona!*

Although she was a girl, she didn't need a penis for courage. *Aquí y donde quiera*, she was ready for a fight.

Those *fregazos* earned her the nickname Margarita *la pajarita*—the birdie girl. But if you called her that to her face, you were in for the worst trouble of your life. We didn't call her that in her presence, only behind her back. With her equals, she was quite capable of taking out her claws and defending herself.

Felisa: *Güera ojos borrados*

With her birth, Felisa tilted our multicolor family to the Spanish side. Fourth in line after me, second to Mague, she took María de Jesús's place, the third-born sister who died an *angelita*. Everybody thought Felisa was beautiful: "¡Mira que bonita!" Because she was very fair: "¡Está tan blanquita!" With blond hair—"¡Ay, que cabellera tan rubia!"—the color of corn silk, she drew everybody to touch her as if her head was holy water. Everybody fussed over Felisa: "¡Qué bonita! ¡Qué güerita!"

As I was on the darker side, I took these comments to heart. I had always believed that our family preferred *güeros*. But with Felisa's birth I was sure.

It wasn't too long before Felisa joined Mague *en sus andanzas*. Whereas Mague liked trouble and the punches that came with it, Felisa would help the one who was hurt but not before getting in her licks.

Consuelo, *la quemada*, who was adopted by the town as a charity case, was one of those people who became Felisa's project. Severely disfigured and scary looking, Consuelo had been badly burned in a fire that destroyed her meager possessions. But she didn't frighten my baby sister.

Abandoned by her husband, Consuelo was left with the responsibility for feeding, clothing, and caring for her many children. Nobody felt pity for her like Felisa.

One time, Felisa raided our standing closet and gave away the clothes our parents had sent from the *yunaitis*. She didn't think we needed them, so she didn't ask for permission to give them away: "Nosotros no necesitamos la ropa como Consuelo y su familia. Al cabo que nos pueden comprar más."

Consuelo and her family came first in Felisa's mind because our parents could always get us more. And we didn't need the clothes as they did.

In one of Consuelo's begging rounds, the four-year-old Felisa gave away our brand-new *pascuas* clothes from the *yunaitis* while we were in school one day. That Easter Sunday Consuelo's kids stood out in our new clothes! We didn't look bad ourselves. We wore new outfits proudly sewn by Tía Herme. She put special effort into rewarding Felisa's generosity—so much so that we looked even more duded-up than la *quemada*'s children did.

Felisa was right. We could always get more, and we did.

Sodas and Coca-Colas

As little as she was, Felisa liked the taste of beer. However, she and my mother didn't have the same appreciation for it. Mother hated to drink— despised the taste and what it did to our father. But with four of her pregnancies, our mother was forced to drink a beer a day. Prescribed by Dr. López to stop her morning sickness and the nausea that wouldn't go away until she gave birth. Mom drank her prescribed beer a day as religiously as praying her rosary. By the faces she made, I could see that she disliked alcohol. But drinking beer was the only way she could keep food in her stomach.

Drinking that beer must have been a big sacrifice for our mother. Wonder if she hated herself when she drank? Wonder if she felt like a drunk? After her pregnancy with Felisa, I never saw her drink again.

Many a time, Mother expressed concern that Felisa's taste for beer was a consequence of her one-beer-a-day prescription. Expressing concern about how this could affect my sister, Mother recalled the day Felisa came in to Tía Herme's store with a fistful of *centavos*: "Qué vergüenza me dió el día que vino Felisa a comprar una soda con tu tía. Como de costumbre, estabamos todas ahí platicando. Felisa llegó con algunos centavos, y pidió una soda. 'Tía, deme un soda. Tengo dinero.'"

As she told me, her face still became a crimson color with the shame. With a fistful of coins, Felisa had come to Tía Herme's store during their adult circle of conversation. Felisa wanted a soda because she had the money to buy one.

Recalling when Tía Herme pulled out a Coke from the icebox, Mom mouthed Felisa's unhesitating response: "'No. No una de esas. De las otras. De las que tomán los grandes.' Can you believe your little sister had the gall to ask for a soda, meaning a beer, like the adults drink?"

Recalling the laughter from adults who thought Felisa's appetite for beer was cute, Mother said, "It didn't help when they laughed. It also didn't help that those men encouraged her by giving her sips."

She recalled saying, "No le celebrén." She didn't want the adults to egg her on.

She never said this to me, but I imagine that our mother must have worried that her one-beer-a-day prescription could have made alcoholics of her children. She wouldn't have forgiven herself if Felisa or any of us had become *borrachas*.

Loss of Innocence

Felisa told me that Father began to touch her when she was eight years old.

Music was Felisa's salvation. But not just any music. Cuco Sánchez, Javier Solís, Chelo Silva, and Lydia Mendoza were but some of the angels that sustained her. The music of México kept her alive.

During the times that Father molested her, Felisa left her body. Went to Tabasco. Returned to Tía Herme, to the things that were home. Don Loro. Pepe. *La tienda* and the *chiles* with saltine crackers. Tuerta was home. Home. The Plaza. Smell of the *pan dulce* and *chicharrones*. Her friends were around her, running and screaming in the streets, calling for her to come out and play. "Vente a las canicas." *Acualaistas. Pepitas. Travesuras.* Home where she felt precious and loved.

The Loving Spoonful and the Beatles, or even the Motown stars, could not be the cure that she needed.

> *No soy monedita de oro*
> *pa' caerles bién a todos*
> *así nací y así soy*
> *si no me quieren ni modo.**

Cuco Sánchez let her pretend that it was not happening to her. That it was not her fault. For a moment she became a famous singer in the movies. It wasn't Felisa. She wasn't being touched after all.

He tried to tell her that he was doing it out of love. But she knew it was wrong. Confused because it felt good, she wanted him to stop. A father doesn't do this to his daughters. He doesn't tell them to keep it a secret. He doesn't play those types of games.

> *Reloj no marques la horas*
> *porque mi vida se apaga*
> *ella se irá para siempre de mi*
> *yo sin su amor no soy nada.*†

She wished she knew all the words to every song. Still, half-learned songs soothed her.

> *Payaso*
> *eres solo un payaso.*‡

It felt as if his touching never stopped. He threatened to hurt the family, Mother, and me especially. I felt scared. I knew he could really kill me.

---

* I am not a piece of gold / to be fancied by everyone / that's how I was born and how I am / if you don't like me, so what.
† Clock, stop tracking the hours / because my life is ending / she will leave me forever / without her love I am nothing.
‡ Clown / you're just a clown.

I saw him beat Mother after touching us. It was his way of showing me that he was serious about what he said. I thought he would kill us all.

Mal hombre
tú no eres nada
ni siquiera un hombre
Mal hombre
tú no tienes nombre
*eres un canalla, eres un malvado.**

Making up new words to Lydia Mendoza's song, she played it over and over in her mind like a broken record. The writer could not even begin to imagine what the words in that song meant to me. *Mal hombre . . . Mal hombre . . . Mal hombre . . .* She repeated the words, trying to put the blame where it belonged. He was the devil: *¡era el chamuco!*

Uno de estos días las otras se irán. Tú te quedaras conmigo porque eres mi favorita. Told Felisa the other girls would disappear one day. And she would be the only one left. With him. Because she was his favorite.

There were other songs. Carried them like baggage attached to her body.

When that didn't work, she just pretended. In the safety of her *pueblo*, she was better able to endure his evil ways.

Juegos y juguetes

Claiming to have fingers of silk, Felisa would remember playing marbles in Tabasco. Her nimble digits were a source of pride. She had shown up the boys. Having knocked out most of the marbles, she was always declared the winner. After her victory, Felisa paraded her jar of marbles for days, like a champion boxer carrying her prized belt, bragging about her

---

* Evil man / you are a nothing / not even a man / Evil man / you have no name / you are rabble / you are evil.

wins. "No que no. También nosotras podemos jugar canicas. Pos' tenemos dedos. No tiene chiste apuntar y darle a las otras."

Thought we couldn't play marbles, huh? Took us for granted, huh? Well, we have fingers too, don't we? It's no big deal to aim and hit the marbles.

Boys didn't think girls could play the game. But she could always sucker them into playing. She saved her money to buy the best tops and marbles, especially the boulders that looked like a big glass eye. The boys had no idea she practiced her shots. Proved them wrong every time. Beat their best player.

She put all the marbles at the center of a large circle that was drawn on the dirt, keeping only the *zarcos*, the hazel-colored ones with specks of blue, brown, and green—those were the chosen weapons. She picked who would go first. After this she took each marble one by one, leaving the circle empty. To win, she had to hit the marbles outside the boundaries. Sometimes she lost her turn, when the boulder stayed inside the circle. Other times her boulder stayed inside, and she lost it to the boy or girl who could hit it out of the circle. She hated that. She usually came out the winner, even though she was the youngest of the girls.

After her victories it was hard to get the boys to play with her. But when they saved enough money to buy new marbles, they challenged her again.

Eyes peeled, they cocked their heads, swaying themselves from side to side, stretching their bodies to look taller in an effort to intimidate her into another game. Pointing the "you-stupid-girl" finger like a water gun, they screamed for *la revancha*. Wanted vengeance. But they really just wanted their marbles back.

If that didn't work, they conned her into playing tops. Spitting on the point and at the end of the string, she tightly wound the top. *Uno. Dos. Tres.* All threw their tops at the same time.

The tops began to spin. Picked up the tops by the palms. Still spinning, passed the tops to another. Back to the ground, still spinning. The top to stop last was the winner. *¡Chihuahua!* Felisa never lost at any game. You'd think they'd be on to her.

In the worst of times, the boys would try to split Felisa's top in half, using the iron post as a weapon. When they succeeded, she ran home. She never cried in front of them. Didn't want the boys to call her a *chillona*, although she had every right to cry.

Playing tops was like dealing with Father. He was the bully with the post who ripped her apart every time he touched her.

Depravities in the House

She said she could fly. Learned about it when Mague told Felisa that she had a magic way to get away. And Felisa later told me.

Bouncing from cloud to cloud, nine-year-old Mague would slip away from the torture. Skipping from one cloud to the next, she'd imagine her sisters and her friends up there with her. Playing hide-and-go-seek, *beísbol*, and Hula-Hoop with a hoop made of tiny clouds, ever so light, easy to balance. Up in the clouds Mague would pass the time.

When we'd play, she was often the one who would ask us to search for figures in the clouds. It was one of Mague's favorite things to do. She was so good at her own game; we could never equal the images that she found.

When he did things to her, Mague went up to the clouds.

Visited the clouds often. Wished she could stay forever. Never come back. Have it all go away.

Noise, voices, or smells pulled her back. Had no choice but to return.

Four years after Mague's trips to the clouds began, Felisa barged into Mom's bedroom. Looking for something. She didn't know what. Walked in on them. Father had Mague pinned against the wall, in a Christ-like pose, with arms spread out and her legs uncrossed. Naked from the bottom, she didn't have a loincloth.

Mague didn't know why she came home, left her sixth-grade class for no reason at all. But Felisa must have suspected something.

This was not like her.

Mother was not at home. Pregnant again, she had gone to her doctor's appointment. He was alone with Mague. No one was there to protect her. Maybe this was the reason why Felisa returned.

Felisa thought I was the only one. She never let herself imagine that Mague was going through worse experiences.

Felisa wished that the earth would open up and swallow her whole. Called for the memory of Tía Hermelinda to protect her. Wanted to run. Go some place other than where she was. But no one was there. She was alone.

Threw herself on the bed and sobbed for Mague, for Mother, and for herself. He was *podrido*, rotten to the core—wasn't even any room for the worm.

Crying didn't make it go away; only the shapes and designs she created in the ceiling of her room gave her comfort. When even that didn't work, she fell on her knees and prayed to the God she believed had abandoned her. But prayers didn't solve her problems.

When Felisa barged in, Father didn't even stop to threaten her with a *monda*. Didn't even hit her; he was so consumed with Mague that he could have cared less what Felisa saw, even though she was only twelve. What he was doing to Mague warned her of impending doom. She could be next. There were no clouds that would protect her and no music that could save her. He would get her.

Felisa later told me she thought of ending it all. But she didn't want to give him the satisfaction. And, like me, she was too frightened to kill him—but wished she could.

La princesa de las nubes rosas, my sister Mague, could always pretend to float away in her pink clouds. Felisa would find her own way.

Still, in our longing for a good father, we felt jealous of the attention Mague was given. Never imagined the price she paid.

The Storybook Daughter

Mague had always been the favorite, the one with the ideal shape and the perfect face. Not yet thirteen, she started to get fat.

Good. For a change someone else would be the fat one. I would gladly abdicate my throne for her.

The storybook daughter, who helped Mother with the kids, was gaining weight. She, who didn't talk back, was becoming quieter. The one who helped in the kitchen was putting too much salt on the food or ruining what she cooked. The favorite daughter was careless with the wash, staining the whites. Still, the ideal daughter continued to do everything a wife was expected to do.

Her mood changed. Chalked it up to grumpiness.

Sometime during the summer of '62, we were forced to move again. Had no clue why.

It was a surprise to all of us, but not to our father.

Soon after the birth of my baby sister Sonia, Father sent Mother and his brood away again. As always, she did what she was told. Packed our belongings. She and her children left for México. Didn't ask questions. Did as she was told.

After a three-day train ride that took us along the coast of México, we ended up in Guadalajara. Arrived at Colonia Agua Azul. Stayed at Tía Chayo's house until we found a home in Belizario Domínguez.

Mother wasted no time enrolling us in school. Younger children entered a public one nearby, and I went to private school. Finally completed the sixth grade. Because of our constant moves, it took three attempts.

Didn't stay long at our aunt's. Had a home in less than two weeks. This one was the best one yet. Prettier than any home we had in the United States. The house was built sturdily, with tile floors throughout the interior. Walls painted in dark blue, yellow, and red—the color of blood when exposed to the air—it was the brightest that I'd ever seen. Well guarded, with iron gates for protection. The house was across from a stadium. Heard thousands of fans cheering as they watched las Chivas Rayadas, Guadalajara's professional soccer team.

Don't know if Mother planned it, but our next-door neighbor was a midwife. She was known as Doña Ester. Had a young son who had eyes for my "fat" sister and me.

Embarrassed by her figure and afraid of boys, I think Mague mostly ignored him. Wasn't interested. Didn't care to draw anyone's attention, much less a young man's interest. Had more than she could handle.

I missed our Santa Clara home even though it was old, smelly, and dilapidated. Longed to play with Jessica, my best friend. Didn't even have time to say good-bye. Wished I had my rag dolls, the ones that my *tía* Herme had taught me to make when I had no one to talk to—they held my secrets. Didn't know to whom to turn. They were the only ones who knew.

We soon grew comfortable in that home. Away from Father's grip my family lived a carefree and happy existence. In Guadalajara we became children again. Played. Ran. Went to the community center to swim and to make friends, with Mother's blessings. We were free again.

As time passed, Mague expanded around the middle. Never spoke about her *panza*. All of us pretended it wasn't happening, including Mother. Blamed her eating habits. Felisa stayed away from her. She thought Mague had an illness *contagiosa*, and she didn't want to catch it. Why does she look like a *bombilla?* Felisa was afraid that she also would turn into a Chinese lantern.

While I went to school, Mague barricaded herself inside the house. As her weight increased, so did her isolation. She didn't want to be seen. Hardly went out of her room. Shame kept her hidden—away from everyone.

The time came when I could no longer pretend it was her weight.

"You're going to have a baby! Aren't you?"

Mague didn't answer. Eyes cast to the floor, she wouldn't look at me. Her body seemed to be shaking as if to get away from itself and me.

"I know whose it is."

After all, she was a pregnant twelve-year-old! What else could she do? Didn't have to speak the horrors to know them. Like Mague, I was afraid of losing my mother and my family.

"But don't tell Mom, okay? She will die."

Mague finally burst out crying. Didn't want her to get upset, so I helped to dry her tears. I was good at that anyway, good at keeping secrets and not too good at touching. I wanted to hug her, but my arms didn't know how. All I could do was touch her with my fingertips and let her know that I loved her. Not knowing what else to do, I let her be.

In a pact of silence, we said nothing. We kept the secret.

Didn't want to kill Mom with our secret. But she must have known, we said to ourselves inside our head without telling each other. Didn't have to talk to suspect. We made up a name, in case someone asked. Mague and I made a pact not to tell who the father was. Mother never said anything or asked any questions. She was still under his spell.

The day finally came. The children were sent to Tía Chayo's, except for me.

I came home from school to hear the commotion. Even though I wanted to help, *las mujeres* didn't let me near the room. Was told to stay out. Anxious and scared, I wanted to do something. Didn't know what to do. Had only witnessed births of animals. Afraid for Mague, all I could do was stay out of the way—curled up in a ball in the corner by the kitchen where I could still keep my eyes glued and my ears wide open.

My little sister who had done everything right and did all she was told was giving birth to a child. She was in hellish pain. Could hear her hollering. Sounded like the cries of death I heard when Father killed a goat for his parties. How could she expel something out of her stomach? She was barely five feet tall and had never weighed more than 100 pounds. Must have felt as if her bones and muscles were coming undone. Her screams lasted forever. Could hear the midwife give instructions. Asked Mague to push. Sent Mother to get boiling water and more towels. Asked Mague to hold it. Told her to pant. With every order that came,

Mague screamed. Her screams sounded like those of the crowd being chased by Frankenstein, her favorite movie. Wondered how Mague felt. Did Doña Ester think Mother was a bad parent? How could Amá stand all of this? Mother was seeing the birth of her husband's lust and violence in her own daughter.

His vile words were useful at a time like this. I found myself using his cuss words, too. *¡Hijo de la chingada!* How could you have done this to my sister? What kind of man does that? You animal! You beast! You inhumane piece of nothing! *¡No vales nada!*

After a long while her baby was born. Named him Juan after our father, just as we agreed. Gave him the name of Carlos as an apology, to cleanse him for the first one. We were just kids, branding him with the name for shame or with a call for help. But nobody heard.

Mague was glad her child was a boy. He would not be put through the betrayal as we had. He would be spared.

Mother never cried. She never said a thing. Kept everything inside, even her pain. Though she didn't talk about it, I could see it in her face. Her eyes had a faraway and distant look that made you want to cry. And she almost disappeared, swimming from the hurt in her already small dresses. Taught my sister how to breast-feed. Already Mague did things grown women do—like take care of children, do house chores, and service my father. Mom had made Mague the loose woman he thought we all were, even though she was really just an innocent child wanting to play with dolls. Mague's son was proof of that.

With another mouth to feed, our family left Guadalajara the summer of 1963. Wished something bigger than us would make us stay, but no one did.

Although we were there only one year, Guadalajara still felt like a sigh. Free of Father's violence and away from his presence, we wanted to stay. But he dictated our movement. We lived subject to his whims.

Gang of One

Back in the United States, we stayed in East Los Angeles for about a year. *De guate-mala a guate-peor*, things went from bad to worse. "Mad" was my nickname, and I wore it well. Moved into the only place where we could find housing. It was where gangbanging got its start, but I had survived worse.

Living in the middle of *hollo Mara*, I could've been recruited into street life had the right person come along. Pent up inside our two-bedroom duplex with a bunch of kids running around, lacking the privacy so many of my friends had, I could easily have been plucked into the streets by the right person. I was a *polla* for the taking. I had the looks. Anger and defiance were my mask. Mouth clenched, pursed lips, I walked around with a hippo-size chip on my shoulder and a scowl no one could have matched.

I could easily have melted into their gangbanger pot. Even wore the clothes they donned. Got their lingo down pat.

But the *vida loca* wasn't meant for me. They hated *wets* and Mexicans like me. Didn't need to apply. Fear of losing my family scared me into not seeing them as an option. Instead of being seduced into gangs, I continued thrashing in the cesspool that was my home. If not for my love of school and books, I would have become a *pachuca*.

Instead, as a fifteen-year-old, I became a gang of one. Still tried to protect my sisters by mouthing off, challenging him, daring him to take me on—short of killing him. As the *bocona, resongona, testaruda* eldest sister who thought she could take him on, I was responsible for their safety. Took it seriously. It was my job.

The warfare at our home was between him and me. Tried to outwit him every way I could. Eagle-eyed him. Plotted his demise to no one but me. To evade his wrath, I pacified him and tricked him, went against him and told my younger sisters not to listen to him as I made them follow my instructions. Challenged him to give himself away when he tried to find my sisters and I had told them to scatter.

"Andele. Busquelas. Si no creé que estan. Encuentrelas." Under my breath, "Stupid, *pendejo*. If you want them, you go find them."

Thought of killing him again and again.

My brothers were spared. They had his protection. Though even they suffered from his violence, but in a silent way. They saw Mother and my sisters beaten for no reason at all. They were victims, too. Sometimes he used their mischief to blame us girls. Made us pay for it.

It was then that Mother became his main target. He beat her when he felt like it. She tried to protect us, but it only made things worse for her and for us girls. Father unleashed every inch of his hate. Ridiculed her. Called her ugly names. Beat her. Then my father would use these beatings to defeat us into submission.

Mother did what she could to protect us. Paid the price with her body and her mind. When she tried to stop him, he turned on her.

"No vales pa' nada, ¡chingada vieja!"

In front of us he told her she was a good-for-nothing.

Wham! The sofa makes a dent on the wall. *Crack!* The glass falls on the floor. *Push!* She almost trips on one of the boys. *Slap!* Her neck jerks to the side and back. *Shove!* He hasn't had enough yet.

Numbed into silence, she was a walking mute. He controlled her every move, like a hypnotist in a circus show. My mother became the unwilling partner in his act. We were his captive audience and his marionettes.

Living in my family as a teenage girl, I felt like a mother and a gang lord all at the same time. Protecting. Fighting. Hiding. Running. Protecting. Fighting. Hiding. Running scared. Fighting mad. I was ready to take on anyone.

Don't know what would have happened if we had stayed in Los Angeles. All I know is that we returned to Santa Clara a year later—not to start anew and make things better, but to continue the same story in a familiar place.

Hijo del aire

Counting the months in reverse, I figure he must have impregnated my sister Mague when Mother was in the hospital having my fifth sister. Sending us to México gave him time to make up a story, create an alibi for his crime. He had three months to know she was not having a period. Wanted the evidence out of the way.

Quiso colgarle el milagro al hijo del compadre, tried to pin the miracle on his *compadre*'s son, Enrique. Didn't stick. Young man wasn't around long enough to get her pregnant. And when he was there, he was never alone with Mague. Wasn't interested in her, anyway. Enrique had a *gringa* girlfriend he wanted to marry. She would fix his papers.

Don't know when Father decided to blame a teacher. Just said one of them, whose name I had never heard before, was at fault. Learned about it when we returned to Santa Clara.

Hearing it enough, Mother almost believed it. Accepted his lies. Seeing otherwise would have broken her world apart.

After Juan Carlos was born, my father vilified Mague, who was now thirteen. Made her out to be a whore. Blamed Mother for having raised her daughters the wrong way. It was her fault she had loose girls.

"Mira que clase de hijas estas criando. Raising whores who pretend to go to school, when all they're doing is having sex. And with their teachers!"

El hijo del aire, he who came from the air—Juan Carlos's arrival stopped my father from ever raping Mague again. He no longer forced her to go to the store. Maybe it was because she was now a mother. Found another target. He now tried to take Felisa instead. But Mague often volunteered, rather than let our baby sister Felisa go with him. It was Mague's way of undermining his despicable plans.

"Get ready. You're going to the store with me."

123

These words were enough to launch Mague into action. She knew what the store translated to: a trip to the foothills and a code for rape.

Mague hated the foothills of East San José and the rolling hills of Milpitas. That's where he took her when they went to the store. He could do what he wanted, with no one to defend her.

To stop her, with her newfound strength, from interfering, our father tried to use Juan Carlos as his ticket. Her son became his biggest pawn. But he didn't realize that in her newly awakened mother's heart, she would have given her life to protect him. Or maybe he suspected that much, because he tried to manipulate her protective instincts by threatening her to stay out of his affairs. There were times my father tried to beat two-year-old Juan Carlos for no reason at all. It was her price for resisting and protecting Felisa, for getting in the way. Despite protests or excuses, Mague continued her battle. She did not let my sister go to the store. Took her place instead.

If I close my eyes, I can still imagine the ways Mague loved and tended to her son, claimed he gave her a reason to live. Loved him just as she had loved her dolls. She held him, cooed to him, and carried him on her hip wherever she went, until he was ready to walk. But, even then, she never let him out of her sight.

Having Juan Carlos didn't stop Mague's penance. It gave my father license to find other ways to abuse her and keep her in her place. If I close my eyes, I can still see the hate in her face as if I were looking in the mirror. There were times that hate made Mague contemplate murder—disappear him from our lives—just as the others had.

🐲 Murder on My Mind

Lo odio. Lo odio. Lo odio. Lo odio. Lo odio. ¡Lo odio! ¿Lo odio?

I hate him. Hate him. Hate him. Hate my father.

When he lived with us, there wasn't a day that I didn't imagine killing him. Often wished I had been strong enough to murder him and to put us out of our misery. Hated him for what he did to my sisters and me. Despised him for what he put my family through all those years. Loathed him for what he did to us. Abhorred him for what he did to my mother.

But I never had the resolve to kill him. Wish I had.

The closest I came was the day I first placed aspirin in his beer after he sent me to get him a drink. I don't recall how many aspirin, but they made him go to sleep. After this, I volunteered to get his beer whenever he asked for one, knowing I had a weapon that would spare us from his demands for that night.

The day I almost killed him, Father had come home already drunk. Mother had made dinner. As was his expectation, we waited for him to eat. It wasn't because he wanted to have dinner with his nice family. He fancied himself so privileged that he didn't want to eat leftovers. Wanted to savor the food before anyone.

Feeling particularly strong that evening, I protested his treatment of my mother. Maybe it was the way he talked to her. Maybe he slapped her because the food was cold. Could've been he threw the food at her because it was salty.

"Deje a mi madre. ¡No le pegue!" Boldly, I told him to stop hitting her. Leave her alone.

"Chingada muchacha. ¿Qué se creé?"

Jumping out of the chair and screaming at the top of his lungs, he lunged forward to slap my face. Seeing his hand come in my direction, I jumped back and ran from him, as he asked who the fuck I thought I was. Because he was drunk, his aim was not particularly good that night. Evaded his slap. Running to the kitchen counter, I pulled a butcher knife from the drawer. Wasn't sure I would use it. Just wanted to have the option if he came at me. Ran outside gripping the knife so fiercely that it seemed to melt into my hand—my anger gave it life.

He followed me. I hid. Ready to pounce on him and stab him if he came near me.

Seeing him in myself scared me, and I ran inside the shell of a broken refrigerator to hide. Stupidly drunk, it was hard for him to walk. Couldn't find me. Prayed he would reach me. He passed near me. Didn't see me. He gave up, having had enough. Ended the search. Went inside. On the alert, I was ready to plunge my weapon into the void that was his heart.

In a daze I restrained myself from going inside the house. I wanted to do him in right at that moment. The idea kept me awake. Didn't think about the consequences. I just wanted to end it all.

Maybe I was prepared to go to jail. Maybe we all were. It would have been better than what we lived. Wanted to kill him. Stopped myself, afraid that my mother, sisters, and brothers would end up starving. Didn't want to break up the family. I couldn't bring myself to do it. I couldn't kill him.

What would have happened to my family? Who would have taken care of my mother?

I must have fallen asleep with the wait. The next thing I remember was Mague asking me to go inside the house. Rousing me, she gently took the knife away from me. I wonder if she felt the same way because she feared I would really do it.

"Give me the knife. He's asleep. Come on, Sister; we'll be okay. Let's go to bed."

I didn't have the guts. Sometimes I wish I had. Once again, we went on pretending that it wasn't as bad as it really was.

Far from the Tree

No one was better than my brothers at playing hide-and-go-seek, especially if they didn't want to be found. Tomás was the best.

My brothers were *super traviesos*, mischievous and rambunctious. They climbed trees. Gave each other nicknames. Ernesto became Cheetah because he liked to play Tarzan. Tomás became Panzas because of his round belly. Juan became Johnny Quest from the cartoons.

Using towels as capes, they often played Superman and Tarzan, jumping from the roof of the carport that stood in the backyard. They started grass fires that got them in trouble for the first time and only because the neighbor complained. Boys will be boys was the apology offered by my father.

Father gave them special treats. Let them watch TV programs we could not. They were able to run around without restrictions.

They could do no wrong.

Father blamed the girls for their mischief, claiming we had failed to watch after them. They became excuses for whippings. Brothers received bribes as ransom for tattling—toys, cookies, and other treats we never had, such as candies, *chicharrones*, and *pan dulce*.

Despite the special treatment they had from my father, we doted on our baby brothers. Along with worrying about our safety, we also had to be concerned about their behavior. Even though their presence added to our burden, we loved them. Wanted them to grow up and be different from our father.

When they were younger, Mother attempted to match each girl to a brother according to rank. Mague and Felisa dutifully accepted the charge, wanting to help Mother with the responsibility.

But I told her no.

"No son mios. Yo no los hice. ¡Cuidelos usted!"

Told her it was not my responsibility to mother my brothers. She had them. They were hers to deal with, not mine. I had other things to do. Books to read. Homework to do.

Still, if they got in trouble, it was always our fault. If they broke something, the girls caused it. Anything they did that could potentially get them in trouble, we sisters were held responsible for. Paid the consequences. The boys lived in my father's hacienda of privilege where *las hijas de Juan* tended to them like servants. From him they learned that women were to be bossed around—bred to serve men.

Eight-year-old Juan, almost-seven Ernesto, and about-to-be-six Tomás—they were too small to protect us and too caring to be like him. But they were quick to run away when he pulled out his belt or cursed at three teenage girls who were seventeen, fifteen, and thirteen. They didn't want to get it. It hurt them to see us treated this way. Often saw tears in their eyes, though they tried to hide them.

I don't know what Juan, Ernesto, and Tomás saw or understood. He bought their loyalty with trinkets. They were drawn to him only when he brought them goodies. Otherwise, they stayed in their playland. He taught them to tattle on us and to get us into trouble. Rewarded them for it. They learned not to be on his bad side. They survived.

Don't know what my brothers saw. But I think they witnessed more than they care to remember. Even though they were small, I know they still recall the time I challenged him to a drinking bout.

Borracheras

The ripped toenail, the refrigerator, those instances were nothing compared to that time I challenged him to drink. Drunk, his brutality had no bounds. I was fed up with him. Someone had to stand up to him. And that someone had to be me. I dared him to a drinking *mano-a-mano*. Wanted to prove to my father that his drinking was not the reason for his hating us so much.

In my own way I was trying to find out if he had a heart. Wanted to know if he had a conscience. Did he realize that he was hurting us? Did he care?

Friday night is here again. He's home again drunk to the gills, making a racket and throwing his weight around.

"It's only an excuse that you don't remember," I say to him with the desperation of a fourteen-year-old who has grown a turtle hide for protection.

"You pretend you don't remember. You hide behind your drinking. You do what you want when you want. Let's see how much of a man you really are. ¿No, qué es muy macho?"

Pulling out a fifth of vodka from the cabinet where he kept his liquor, I tell him, "I'll show you. I'll remember everything. *¡Ándale! A ver.* Let's see who wins."

My mother attempts to stop it. She takes the bottle away from my hand.

He backhands her. Knocks her on the floor. Tells her to sit. Be quiet. Stay out of it.

"*¿Qué te importa?*"

Tells her it's none of her business. Accuses her of jealousy.

"*¡Cochina! Celosa ¿de tu propia hija?* You're just jealous because your own daughter wants to drink with me," he gloats as he takes on the challenge.

Good thing we finished eating before it all began. I hated the smell and taste of alcohol. Had to force myself to gulp the stuff. I hated alcohol maybe as much as I hated him. It reminded me of the whippings he gave us when he was plastered. Despised the pickled vinegary smell that seeped from his pores and made him smell like rancid cabbage. Sometimes he smelled of vomit.

We begin the challenge.

Following the swig with everything that was going on around us. Numbering every drink we take, taking the first three in stride.

"*Esta es la cuarta copa y ahí va su hijo corriendo de miedo.* Your boys are so afraid of you that they run when they look at you. *Quinta.* My mother's tears are running down her face. She's too afraid to tell you how horrible you really are." *Sexta.* Mague peeks in to see if I'm okay. *Séptima.* Mother is looking at me as if she wants me to stop drinking. I ignore her, and I don't let her get to me. *Octava.* "You're nodding out. Your face is falling on the kitchen table. You see, I know what's going on around me. I'm not fading out." *Novena.* "You passed out," I say to no one in particular as I pour the tenth one.

Mother takes it from my mouth. "He's out."

He's out. We're free of the monster for the night.

That's the night I gave up drinking for life.

When they saw he was passed out, Mother and Mague took the bottle.

"*Ya parale, Josefina. Está dormido.*"

"Look, Sister. I know everything that's taking place. You and my mother are taking me to the shower. You want, you don't, you want me sober, not drunk. I swear I'll never forget what happened tonight. He has no excuses. Poor excuse for a father. He's no fucking man. He's a fucking coward!"

Mom said, "Los niños y los borrachos dicen la verda." I began to cry as the child who is drunk with truth. Couldn't hold it anymore. Anger was oozing from the bottom of my soles to the tip of my hair. Mague calmed me.

"Shhhh! You'll wake him. Shhhhhhhh! He'll take it out on you. Shhhhhhhhhhhh! He won't be happy to find out you proved him wrong. Shhhh! Be quiet or we'll pay for it." Mague whispered, putting her hand over my mouth to muffle my voice. She was afraid I'd wake him.

After our main bout he continued to do what he wanted when he wanted because he felt like it. He felt it was his right and kept on as if that day had never taken place.

My drinking contest was for nothing. Only thing I learned was that drinking or not, he was the way he was. He would stop at nothing to impose his will.

The Rape of Felisa

It finally happened. He raped Felisa.

About to turn thirteen, Felisa had reached what he must have regarded as her coming-of-age year. He had waited long enough. She was due for her rite of passage. Had been three long years since he had "made a woman out of Mague."

As it was when he raped Mague, Mother was pregnant. This time she was carrying the sixth girl. He decided to name her María del Refugio in memory of his mother. How noble of him!

Guess he liked raping my sisters when my mother was having his daughters at the hospital.

Thinking back to those days, Father had the perfect setup. He was usually home because he went to work in the wee hours of the morning as a garbage man. He came home to his kingdom, a basement that was off limits to all. Ruled it with an iron hand.

He returned from work before we went to school. We long ago had learned to get ready before he arrived home. We didn't want him in our way. Didn't want him peeping.

Father was extra clean. Took a bath as soon as he came from his rounds. Lorded over the bathroom we all used. Kicked us out if we weren't finished. Peeled off his clothes and left them on the floor for Mother to collect. Came out with his pomade-slick hair combed back, every hair in place, smelling of whatever aftershave lotion he rescued from his trashcans.

Scared us when he was so perfumed, a signal that he was up to no good.

Working for Santa Clara Sanitation Company, my father set traps for my sisters, but his lures didn't work. They didn't matter to us. We didn't need or want anything. Only wanted to be left alone.

The day it happened, Mother was in the hospital. Everybody was in school, except for Felisa, who was not feeling well that day.

Father came home. He followed his cleaning ritual and went to the basement.

Called Felisa to come to get something he had picked up for her. She ignored him. She pretended she was finishing homework, or feigned she had something or other to do.

He screamed for her to come down. She refused.

He told her he had something to give her—a jewelry box with a dancing ballerina that played music when it opened.

"I don't need that. What do I want that for? I don't even have any jewelry. And I hate that stupid song." It played *Bolero* by Ravel.

"Keep your trinket. I don't want anything from you," Felisa told him.

Insisting she come down to the basement, he promised other things. Felisa refused.

She hated that place—*ese maldito lugar de tortura*. It was his torture chamber.

Finally, Father had enough. Tired of the game and leaving a trail of Hai Karate, the trendy cologne of the year before, he walked outside, into the main house, and he came through the back door.

He dragged Felisa into the basement. Kicking. Screaming. Cursing up a storm. With all the strength she could muster, she fought him. Called for God's help, but it didn't come. None of her kicks landed on him.

Felisa had just taken a bath. She was still dressed in her school clothes. Her fear of him didn't stop him. It excited him. Aroused even more by her resistance, he began to rip off her clothes.

Told her today was the day he would make her a woman.

"Ahora te toca. Te voy hacer mujer."

As if it was an obligation, he uttered, "It's your turn. I will now make you a woman."

Felisa didn't make it easy for him. She continued to resist. She fought him. Screamed. Scratched. Hit. But her struggle was to no avail. He finally forced himself on her, tearing her insides into pieces until the mattress he kept in the basement became soaked—with her blood.

Felisa felt as if she had been stabbed with a dull knife; her insides were on fire. She trembled like an earthquake. She tried to shake his evil from her. How could he? He was supposed to be her father who loved her. This was not love. The monster had swallowed her whole and spit her into nothingness, worthlessness.

When he was done, he left her there. Like a hurt animal run over by a car, she was left to tend to her wounds. She doesn't remember how long she was in the basement. Felisa pieced together the filthy clothes he had torn to shreds. Covering herself as best she could, she dragged her body from the basement up the stairs, out the door, to the backyard, and up the stairs again into the house, hoping that no one would see her. Every part of her body hurt and shook, like the ice in the blender when he made his *margaritas*. Everyone would be home from school soon. She didn't want them to find her in such a state.

I don't know how many times he raped her. She told me she showered three times. The water didn't help, though. She felt despicable. Blamed herself. Thought she had caused it with her beautiful body. Didn't tell anybody. Kept it to herself. Didn't even tell Mague.

Home from the hospital, my mother noticed fingernail scratches on his face. She asked him about them. Father lied. He blamed them on work. He claimed the thorns on a bougainvillea tree were too close to a garbage can he emptied.

Putrid, like the stench of the garbage cans he emptied, he continued to impose himself. He still tried to drag Felisa to the store whenever he felt the urge.

Feast of the Monster

"Leave him alone! He's only a child! You horrible man!"

Mague was holding on to her little son for dear life. Father was yanking at him as if they were playing tug-of-war, trying to strip Juan Carlos away from her arms. The boy was screaming and kicking and yelling. No no no! That's all he could say; he was only two.

I knew he was hurting Juan Carlos, so I ran out of the house. I screamed at him to stop it.

Ignored me, as if I wasn't there. Wrapped in his own rage, he wasn't even aware I was there. Father pushed Mague to the ground, finally nabbing Juan Carlos from her arms. Juan threw him in front of the family car that was backed up into the driveway. Ordered him to stay. Threatened him with a whipping. Like a scared deer, Juan Carlos froze on the spot.

"¡Chingadas cria! Muchacho pendejo, no se mueva. ¡Quedese ahí! Si se mueve, lo jodo."

The threat of a beating if he didn't stay still or if he moved froze Juan Carlos on the spot. His only defense was to cup his ears with his tiny hands as he tried to stop Juan's slurs from invading his ears. Although muffled, he still heard "Fucking kid. Stupid child." Shaking like Jell-O, Juan Carlos dissolved into the driveway.

Running to his rescue, Mague and I both grabbed Juan Carlos and pulled him to safety.

"Leave him alone. ¡Dejelo! No le haga nada. ¡Es tan solo un niño!"

Mague knew he had meant to kill her son this time. She pushed Juan Carlos out of the way, just as my father, behind the wheel of the car, sped out in anger, spewing gravel stones all over the walls of our house and the neighbor's house.

Father had meant to run over Juan Carlos. Had not expected us to resist. Thought we would take it, as we had taken everything else.

As he peeled off, he glared at my sister with a look of *ya lo pagarás*, his you'll-pay-for-it warning. That look of revenge we knew well; it told us what was in store for her. Made me realize what he was doing to her. But Mague was able to stop his advances for the first time.

In the trail of his dust, Mague came into the house with her son clinging to her neck. She was crying with the pain of someone who had almost lost her only child.

Juan Carlos, a nervous child who never seemed to have any peace, must have sensed my father's hate for him. I'm sure that my father wished Juan Carlos, the evidence of his betrayal, the son of no one, had never been born. Still continued to use alcohol as an excuse, intensifying his drinking when he didn't get his way or beating on little children to manipulate his wants.

Braggart and Saints

Reeking of alcohol and having spent much of his paycheck, my father was brought home by Compadre Pajaro Reynaga many times. Because my father loved to buy drinks for his pals, he wasted his money as if he didn't have a family to support.

Friday was the day he always went on a drunken spree. He binged until he went to work on Monday, claiming that his *borracheras* didn't interfere with his ability to provide for his family. When it was time for him to come home—and we never knew when that was—my mother and the rest of us walked on eggshells.

Friday nights were *nuestro fín del mundo*, when our world ended. We girls rounded up the younger kids and readied them for bed. We didn't want them around to see the end of the world in our house. We made sure everything was in its expected place, not wanting him to have a reason to hit any of us. In the extra clothes we still continued to wear, we went to bed shaking with the knowledge that one of us would be his prey again. Too late for Mague. I didn't realize he had hurt Felisa, too.

With a *pachuco* appearance and the tattoos of their rebel days, the Reynagas, Pajaro and Mary, had hearts of gold. They took their godparenthood seriously and came to visit the family whenever they could.

Mary was a supersize woman with bright red hair that set off the blue and red colors of her arm tattoos that constituted the souvenirs of her former *vida loca*. She loved Antonio Aguilar, the Mexican *charro*, and even the color aqua because it was his favorite. One year she painted her entire Santa Clara house that same color, to the horror of her *gringo* neighbors. Afraid of her looks and her frank mouth, no one complained. Told her the house looked great.

Pajaro, a slight and dark man with a thick mustache, was given his name because he carried a stuffed hummingbird inside his pocket. He adored Mary. He lived in fear of losing her and carried a dried amulet as insurance for keeping her love. His Indian past told him she would stay if he carried it around with him, come rain or come shine.

Mary and Pajaro were almost always together. Like flesh and nail, *carne y uña*, they were inseparable.

One Sunday after Pajaro had dropped him off, my father finally let down his guard. He started pushing and shoving all of us around, cussing his mouth off, as soon as he entered the house, but this time he didn't care whether it was his boys or the girls. He didn't care that Pajaro was still there to see everything. Later, Pajaro showed up with Mary. They had returned because they were worried about how he was with us, something they had never before seen. Or maybe Mary had been betrayed, too.

After making sure he was calmer and had something to eat, Mary left him with a warning. She told my father she was keeping an eye on him.

"Tenga cuidado, Compadre. ¡Vallase por la sombrita!"

Watch your step, Compadre.

Be careful, she repeated in English for our benefit. She wanted him to know that she had her eye on him. She told him to walk on the shady side of the street, because the shadow he sees might be hers. She intuited that something just wasn't right.

The next day the police showed up at our high school and took Mague. The counselor took her out of class. When Mague saw the police, she knew. Instead of fear she felt thankful to know someone had told. She didn't deny the charges and willingly told her story, not sparing any details. To make her feel safe, the cops told her that Father was in jail. But it didn't matter because she would have told them everything anyway. He had taken everything from her. She had nothing more to fear. What more could he do?

With Mague in the car, the police went to pick up Felisa at her middle school, but they never came for me. Guess my story wasn't bad enough.

Mary Reynaga was our patron saint; she had interceded where no one had. It must have been Mary. It was the day after that weekend binge, and the Santa Clara County welfare department lady told us that a woman who called herself a family friend had called. It had to have been Mary; no one else had the guts.

When I came home from school, everything was in disarray. Mother didn't seem to understand what was happening. Everyone was sobbing, except Felisa, who came running to me. "The secret's out. They know everything and what he did to us. He won't hurt us anymore! They took him away, and he's finally in jail where he belongs. I hope he rots!"

Relieved but still frightened, we were happy to have him gone.

/

While we celebrated, Mother was more concerned with the family's survival. Who would support us? As a family without a provider, how would we make do? She barely spoke English. She didn't know how to drive—he had refused to teach her. She had no trade. All she knew was the fields. He had raised eight children and Juan Carlos. How would she support us?

Que lejos estoy del suelo

donde he nacido

So far from the land that

gave me birth

Released from His Tyranny

We sisters were sure Mary Reynaga told. She of the burgundy hair we now call Mexican Red, who was too tall for a Mexican, the *comadre* who spoke funny Spanish. The one her neighbors had learned to respect because of her strength, despite her I-don't-have-to-please-anyone attitude. The one who loved Antonio Aguilar the Mexican *charro* and anything associated with him. Mary loved him so, she painted her house aqua just because it was his favorite, in the face of middle-class protests in her neighborhood—it was her house, and Mary could do with it what she wanted. Pajaro, her bird of a husband, agreed. And he didn't even protest when Mary carved "Tony," her endearment for him, on her upper right arm to record her love. Mary, that number one fan of the Zacatecano, also must've been eagle-eyed about those things—figured it out and told.

A woman freed us from my father's tyranny. I forever will be grateful to Mary Reynaga for unlocking the door to our freedom.

When the juvenile justice and welfare department workers descended on the school with the police to question my sisters about our family life, even though frightened and intimidated by them, my sisters didn't keep the secret. Feeling protected and free from the burden we had been forced to endure, my sisters could finally tell the truth at the school nurse's office.

My sisters told the truth about our family. And they believed my sisters! They kept us in school until my father was arrested at the house. Shortly thereafter, we were separated from my mother. She was taken to the battered women's shelter with my baby sister, Mary. Mague and Juan Carlos, Felisa, Juan, Ernesto, Tomás, Sonia, and I were taken to the Santa Clara County Children's Shelter. I don't remember how long we stayed, but I think it was about a month.

Our father was taken to the county jail. He was charged, and he had a public defender to protect him. They kept him there until the trial.

No great loss. We were glad he was out of our lives.

Under protective custody at the county shelter, my sisters, brothers, and I awaited our case disposition from the family judge. Six-year-old Tomás, three-year-old Sonia, and two-year-old Juan Carlos were too little to understand. They cried for our mother, but they were easily distracted with toys. They liked the attention they got from the workers, and my younger brothers and sisters soon adjusted to the shelter. They almost looked as if they had left the trauma behind.

In the midst of all the chaos, I was thankful for the possibility of a new life without my father. I wanted us back in our home with Mother at the helm. Wanted to give her a chance to show the love we knew she had for us.

Still, the authorities kept us from her. They wanted to make sure she was fit to parent us. They suspected she was an active part of our abuse. They couldn't understand how all of it could have taken place right under her nose. All were suspicious of her.

The children enjoyed their play. I was grateful my family was out of my father's clutches. Felisa finally felt safe.

The Shelter

Father wouldn't bother us anymore, but he branded us for a lifetime. I lived in the uncertainty of daily life without his dictates, lost in not knowing what was to come. Still we had to deal with it all—*nuestras garritas al aire,* there for all to inspect and dissect.

My stay at the shelter was so traumatic that I only remember walking the halls of the high school in body. I attended classes, but what they were, or who the teachers were, or what the classrooms looked like is open to question. I ambled about *como la mujer llorona* looking for her place in the world.

What lives on is the shame I felt. Dressed in hand-me-downs with boat shoes I wouldn't have been caught dead in, I was a walking target for ridicule. The bus with its Santa Clara County Juvenile Authorities letter-ing that took us to St. Patrick's Catholic Church on Sunday identified us as wards of the court. People's stares deepened my hurt. The pity I saw in their eyes pierced a deeper hole in my heart. And their unspoken ques-tions made the hairs on my skin stand at attention, the goose bumps creating a distance between us. "Why are you here? What'd he do to you? How come you're not in court? Where is your mother?"

My younger sisters and brothers attended school in the shelter. Mague and I went to Andrew Hill High School in San José, forcing our transfer from Santa Clara High School. Mague was in the tenth grade, and I was in the eleventh. I was just as embarrassed to be in a new school and coming from the shelter as I was with anyone finding out about our family history.

I stayed really close to Mague. I didn't make any friends, and people I met there have remained the blur they were then. Neither of us cared to look at boys. We wanted to be left alone. But we had each other.

When we were finally released to Mother's care, my family returned to the house we had on The Alameda. We returned to our old schools. At Santa Clara High, Mrs. Kincaid, the dean of students, welcomed Mague and me. She talked to our teachers and counselors to smooth out the transition and made sure we didn't lose credits. She didn't want us to suffer more than we already had. Took me under her wing.

My grades didn't suffer. By not letting our circumstances affect my grades, I was holding on to my honor. School continued to matter more than ever. Mr. Fiore, Mague's counselor, sought me out and hired me as a student worker.

I asked Ms. Hilje, my counselor, to enroll me in college preparatory courses, though she didn't think I could handle it. After all, Mexicans who are bilingual already had it good enough to become secretaries. They could get out of the heat from the fields and into the shade of clerical work. She tried to talk me into business courses. Still, I made her enroll me in college prep, with a note I wrote for my mother telling her to sign me up in the classes. The challenge became algebra. I had lost my love for math in the sixth grade, when I was forced to do it the American way, working out all the steps instead of solving them in my head.

I worked as Mrs. Kincaid's student assistant. Took attendance for students who had to do detention. Students tried to bribe me to let them off the hook after they cut classes, my sisters included. No one would know. Still, I turned them in just the same as the surfer bums who attempted to be my friends. I made everyone do their time.

During my father's sentencing phase, the judge met with my family— my mother and all of us nine kids. He wanted to offer us a new treatment program. Its emphasis was to keep families together through treatment. The judge was concerned about breaking up our family. Didn't he see we were already a broken one? Why would he want to keep him in our home? Hadn't the judge learned what he did to us? What would happen to my little sisters? No way in hell would I want that.

"Do you want your father to live with you?" he asked every one of us, from the oldest to the youngest. One after the other loudly answered.

Josephine? "No!"

Margaret? "No!"

Felisa? "No!"

Johnny? "No!"

Ernest? "No!"

Thomas? "No!"

Sonia? "No!"

Juan Carlos (who was just three)? "No!"

María, who could not yet talk, was the only exception. But if she could talk, she might have wanted him to stay.

"I don't want to break up your family. Your father could go to treatment. You could stay together." The judge tried to convince us. We almost screamed "No!" letting him know we really meant it. Wanted nothing to do with our father. Better dead than a life with him.

"We want to stay with our mother."

After completing their assessments, the welfare and juvenile authorities decided that my mother was not part of his madness. She was just another victim. They decided we would be safe under her care.

Close to Thanksgiving in 1965, Child Protective Services took us home. My mother was there with our baby sister in her arms, waiting for us. I could read shame in her face, in the slouch of her shoulders and the defeat of her eyes. When she saw us, however, life came into her like a plant that is scorched from thirst and has just been watered. We clung to her, afraid to let go.

"No lloren. Estamos juntos y nadie me los quitará."

I had heard Amá cry in her room before, but now she started to cry for us to see. All of us joined in, realizing that we could have been taken away from her. But there was more pain to come and more tears to shed.

Court Hearings

Nobody took what he did to me seriously. He hadn't hurt me enough.

I didn't go to court. Instead, I took care of the kids.

Mother, Mague, and Felisa had to confront him without me.

He came into the courthouse in his orange jail jumpsuit, shackled in handcuffs with leg irons binding his movement; I saw him from the waiting room. Didn't see me. It was his profile—no one had that nose or that mustache. Could have made him out anywhere. Perfect Roman nose flaring with hate—made that pencil-thin *bigote* of his stand out in the crowd.

For the first time I didn't fear him. Now he was the shackled one, instead of me. Confused between pity and celebration, I grieved for the loss of the father I never had.

Not a witness and underage, I was kept out of the hearing. Couldn't imagine what it was like for *nuestra madre*. Wanted to testify, but I was spared. Didn't have to be poked and prodded by tests and exams as my sisters were. Didn't have to endure their questions in front of all to hear, to pick apart, to doubt.

"I should have trusted my instincts. Pero yo no esperaba esto de tu papá," Amá would now say out loud for us to hear, telling us that she never would have expected this from our own father.

His beatings, his threats, his fondling, his drunken violence, his manip-
ulations, the rapes, and the way he made Mague pregnant must have been
excruciating for my mother to hear. Even though the hearings were in
English, my mother didn't have to know the language to hear the pain.

Thirteen-year-old Felisa was devastated by the interrogations of the
attorneys on both sides. In Felisa's case, it was her word against his. She
was furious about the way my father's attorney tried to confuse her.

"We weren't making up such horrible things. How could they even
think that? We weren't making it up. . . . Mague and I didn't testify at the
same time. I felt as if they were trying to find us in a lie. They were trying
to catch Mague and me in a lie."

Mague's evidence was clear because of her son. Felisa was accused of
making up my father's violations. She was appalled by their legal gymnas-
tics.

"The attorney kept asking the same questions over and over. He
wanted me to trip over my own words. But I could only tell the truth. He
was crazy to think I would make this up."

Felisa told her story over and over again. She felt doubted, accused of
being a liar, judged by all the men who defended my father, and doubted
by all the attorneys on both sides. It was like a rape without touching, she
said.

Charges of promiscuity and seduction were made. They dared to claim
that Father hadn't been the first.

Had she slept with anyone? Did she like having sex with her father?
Who started it? Why didn't she stop it? How come she didn't tell anyone?
Where was her mother? How could she not know? It was happening right
under her nose. Why didn't she do anything about it?

"The most painful thing for me was to see Mom straining to understand what was going on," Felisa told me. "With tears streaming down her
face, it was as if she was feeling the pain alongside me. I couldn't stand to
look at her. I couldn't even look her way." Felisa felt as if she had created
the pain. She didn't want to look at our father. "Me dolía ver el dolor en
nuestra madre."

Felisa and Mague had agreed to stay true to the facts. They were not going to cover up anything. This was the only way he would be out of our family's life. Felisa knew that telling the secret was the only way to protect *nuestra familia*.

Father mocked everything Felisa said.

Me la vas a pagar.

Raising his hand in a motion that warned, "Just wait and see what will happen to you," he laughed at her.

"I was telling the truth. He would finally pay for his sins. For the first time I felt he could no longer hurt me."

The judge sentenced my father to seven years at Atascadero State Hospital, a prison and mental hospital all in one. He should have been sent for life, but he got off easy. Wish I had been there to make sure he was sentenced to more time. I didn't get my time in court. Had more years to add. He should have received at least ten, for those years I lived inside his prison. That would have been fair.

With the court hearing over, the younger children complained for weeks of stomach problems and headaches. We would fight for no reason. We also learned that Amá had a temper. She raged over every little thing.

The way we figured, Amá was finally letting out all the anger she had stored. She wasn't upset at us. It was mostly herself she blamed. It could have been the fear and anger about the way her life turned out, but she never abused us. She did all she could to create a safe environment for us.

With time, and realizing she would be okay, Amá began to relax, to fully mother and tend to us. But we still had to contend with the consequences of his inhumanity in other ways.

Seizure and Release

It was the day of his sentencing that Felisa had the seizure. She fell, shaking like someone had put her inside a blender, on the living room floor.

"¡Felisa! ¡Hermanita! ¡Despierta!"

My brothers and sisters started crying and stepped in as if they could do something for her. Thinking that she was about to die, we all tried to help her. Tripping over each other, yelling and screaming for everyone to get out of the way, and staying in the middle of it all, we called for Amá as we tried to bring her back.

Then I remembered what I had learned in school: roll up a face towel tightly so she doesn't gag on it and put it inside her mouth, to stop her from swallowing or biting her tongue.

Kneeling next to her, I stroked her hair and held her in my arms. I turned away to yell at the kids to quiet them. But they were running in circles, fascinated and scared. I had no idea whether all this would help her, but I tried. Amá took over, and I was released from the duty of being in charge.

After what seemed an eternity, Felisa came out of the seizure.

An ambulance finally arrived.

The medics examined Felisa and took her to the hospital for observation. She was given medication for epilepsy, medication that she never took.

Felisa never had another seizure. It was as if it came to shake off all the ugliness. But it didn't.

Found Out

Felisa and I were *mojadas*. Well, we were really *alambristas*, wire fence jumpers, because in California you cross or jump a fence instead of the river. We found this out with our court hassles. It took almost six years for them to smoke us out, 1959 to 1965.

When my father had finally decided to bring us to the United States in 1959, he took the easy way out because it would have been too hard and too costly to raise the $3,000 bond needed to cross Felisa and me legally. I was to pretend that I was Mague, who was born in Weslaco, Texas. Felisa was *güera* enough, and Father knew they would ask no questions. They didn't. We passed without a fuss.

As my parents were permanent residents, there was no reason to question our status before this entry. Father must have learned all the tricks.

La migra came to our home in the name of John Smith—his real name. He was the agent who came to see about our status. He didn't round us up, only came to write a permit that allowed us to stay. However, with that permit came the restriction that denied our traveling to México. He warned us that if we left the United States, Felisa and I could never return. I wasn't sure I wanted to return.

"No preocuparte," John Smith said compassionately to Amá. "Ellas estar contigo. No tener miedo."

Smith calmed her as he collected our dates of birth, day and year of crossing, and the border site from which we entered. Mr. Smith jotted it on two temporary cards. Gave them to Amá, who put them away for safekeeping and gave them to us when we turned of age. Felisa and I never had to carry those cards. We fit in and no one ever asked. Must have looked *pochas* enough to fit in; no longer *mojadas*, we could pass.

Now we had permission to stay, permission to go to school, and even permission to work if we so desired. However, the federal laws denied us public assistance. We couldn't become charges of the state or we would not have the right of citizenship. Aliens didn't have any right to receive welfare—weren't eligible, had never been. Felisa and I must have been reported when Amá went on welfare.

"Felisa and Josie are not entitled to benefits, and the state has no obligation to support them" because we were *mojadas*. We didn't have the right to welfare, but we had the right to stay.

"You just have to make do."

And she did. Made do with what she received for seven kids. She fed nine.

I memorized our AIs, the alien identification numbers, by heart. Mine: AI 014 703 520. Felisa: AI 014 703 521. If the *migra* happened to stop us, I wanted to be ready. Didn't want to take any chances.

Those numbers gave us rights. We could now be in the open and not be subject to my father's threats of deportation. We had a right to be here. He could do nothing about it. I haven't forgotten those numbers, just as I'll never forget the address and our home on The Alameda.

ᗧ The First Thanksgiving

It has since been demolished to make way for an auto parts store—our address was 3335 The Alameda, Santa Clara, California 95050. The house was between the Vegas, who lived at the corner of the block, and Mr. Luigi, who lived next door. It was just six short blocks away from our elementary school and three blocks away from my dream school, Santa Clara University.

We always returned to The Alameda. The first time was when we left the fields. The second time was when we returned from Guadalajara with Mague and her baby. And the third time was when our father was sent to Atascadero, where sex offenders and predators served their time, condemned to a mud hole for their pig ways.

When my family first arrived at The Alameda, we had no stove or refrigerator. We didn't even have dishes. Ate chili beans, fresh corn, and Campbell's soup heated in tin cans on the coals of the fireplace of our living room. Our house was no mansion. It was a yucky yellow mustard house with brown trim that mirrored our life. The walls of the house were dressed with peeling wallpaper lined with cracks that sheltered the roaches and provided food for the rats. The house reeked of old age and the rotten cheese smell of rat feces, and the ammonia of their urine made our noses burn until we adjusted to the stench.

When my father lived with us, The Alameda's basement was a torture chamber. There he killed goats for *birria* and pigs for *chicharrones*. In that space animals died along with child spirits.

With a cold-blooded expertise, my father took pride in his ability to butcher. Piercing the pig's neck, he leered at my younger sisters, hinting at what they could expect. The pig's squealing was an omen for what they would face.

Now as we returned to The Alameda without our father, the roaches made us feel at home. Looking at each other and without saying a word, we knew we had much to be thankful for—we were together as a family without him.

We had electricity. We had our home.

My sisters and I ran from room to room to make sure that the monster was gone. We checked every crevice. We combed every possible hiding place.

Inspecting the back porch, we tripped on a box of groceries left by the Salvation Army. I guessed the kindly Mr. Brown, our social worker, thought of it. It was Thanksgiving.

"Amá. ¡Aquí hay una caja con comida!"

Amá didn't believe us. The only free food we knew was the bread that my father collected from his garbage rounds.

"There's a box of food on the back porch!"

"Qué comida, ni que nada. ¡Metanse!"

Amá didn't believe us, but we dragged in our newfound treasure.

"¡Mire! ¡Un turkey!"

Up to this time the bird had no meaning to us. Thanksgiving isn't a Mexican holiday, and my father refused to make it one of ours. Now, however, we were happy to celebrate with style, *con un* turkey. We could now be like our other friends, turkey and all.

That first Thanksgiving was the best meal we ever had. We savored canned corn, boxed mashed potatoes, green beans from a can, Langendorf white bread, and store-bought pumpkin pie—things we had never eaten before. Only thing we didn't like was the cranberry jelly. Best of all is that we all sat around the table with our mother, who ate with us for the first time. Didn't have to wait for her to serve everyone; she was there with us.

Now when I pass a Salvation Army collection kettle, I can't go by without giving. The dinging of the coins reminds me that they were there when we most needed them. The feelings we had repressed were slowly coming back. We were thankful to feel and grateful to be able to laugh, as we relearned to enjoy life and share stories.

La Vaquera Tejana: How Mague Learned to Ride a Pig while Playing Hooky

What made that first Thanksgiving meal was the *vaquera* story. Even the boys, who have no memories of México and its enchantments, were rolling on the floor.

When Felisa and Mague were little girls, they loved the *muladar,* an open field where everyone threw their discards. Barely in kindergarten, Felisa talked Mague and a group of their friends into skipping school to go to the *muladar.* They would go scavenging. Searching for treasures, they found jewelry, pieces of crystal, magnifying glasses, and even coins. Already a nerd, I was excluded from the adventure.

"Ándale, Mague, vamos. ¡No seas mala!"

Magic and *muladar* were the same to my sisters. They could get lost in the heap.

A trip to the dump usually meant checking out the neighborhood. My sisters began with a walk to the edge of the Tabasco River, where cousins and friends learned to swim, catch fish, and evade the water snakes. The group would often make a pit stop at Tía Luisa's, who lived near the river's edge and in front of the *muladar.*

After a plate of *quesadillas,* Tía Luisa, who pretended she didn't know they were skipping school, let them continue on their tour. She was always the *alcahueta,* covered for them, backed them up and didn't tell anyone.

They always passed by the Raygoza ranch, a detour, but they wanted to admire the blooming red roses that spilled around the alfalfa field, creating a still life of the orchard. From that high point the *muladar* looked like a piece of art.

It's a good thing Juan José, my father, was in the United States. *¡Diosito!* He would have been *fastidiado* by his daughters' *travesuras*. *¡Qué vergüenza!* What a shame!

Mague, in the name of sisterhood, reluctantly agreed to go to the magic place. She and Felisa loved to play and to make something out of nothing, *de los escombros de otros*. It was not unusual for them to spend a whole day at the *muladar*. It was better than school. Mague, Felisa, and *las chirrionas* could always disappear in the dump.

It was then that Mague finally had a chance to test her *vaquera* roots. She bragged about being a Texan every chance she had. You'd think she was born in the Alamo! Reminded us every chance she was given.

"I am a cowgirl from the state of Texas. ¡Yo soy tejana!"

But the *pinguillas* were not alone at the *muladar*. Also searching for something, a band of *puercos* was looking for something to eat.

Lost in their foraging, neither the children nor the pigs sensed each other until it was too late.

Had it not been for Mague's nature call, the two never would have met.

"Felisa, vámonos. ¡Tengo que hacer el número dos!"

Yelling to Felisa that she wanted to go to the bathroom, Mague demanded to go home. Not yet ready, Felisa pointed to a secluded spot and told Mague to go there.

"¡Ándale! Busca a donde ir. Haz ahí. Ahí 'tá un lugarcito. Bajate los chonis y haz! Go ahead! Find a spot to go. Do it there. There. Do it in that space. Pull down your *chonis* and go."

Despite her urgency to do Number Two, Mague squeezed her cheeks together. Afraid to unload in the open and away from the corral with which she was familiar, Mague waited some more.

She couldn't persuade Felisa to leave. The pickings were good that day.

Shaking from her need, Mague held it. Let her little sister continue exploring. Still too scared to go, Mague waited some more. Then she could wait no longer. She was ready to unload. Took her position, pulled her *chonis* down, and heard the squealing sounds headed in her direction.

Led by the delicious smell of *mojones*, a pack of hungry *puercos* stampeded straight for her *caca*. Seeing them head in her direction, Mague realized that the pigs were aiming for her load. She had forgotten that *puercos* ate shit and *marranos* were raised on feed.

¡Diositio! ¡Son puercos! It's pigs!

Immobilized, Mague prayed to disappear.

With her Harina la Piña flowery cotton panties in hand, Mague ended up mounted on the back of the largest and fastest of the *puerco* pack. In the blink of an eye, Mague became the hog rodeo queen. Finally got a chance to test her Texan roots.

Bronco-riding its back, Mague grabbed on to the pig's ears for dear life. The pig ended up with more than it bargained for. My sister turned out to be a prize-winning cowgirl.

Felisa and her friends were dying from laughter. Chasing after Mague and the horde of pigs, Felisa started yelling and rooting for her Texan sister.

"¡Que viva Mague! ¡Que viva la tejana! ¡Ajua!"

Hollering "Long live the Texan," Felisa made such a ruckus that her screams frightened the pigs away. Mague landed on her butt, *chonis* still in hand.

"¡Que buena eres para montar! Duraste mucho, y lo mejor fue que no tuviste que limpiarte con una piedra. Te cepillaste con el cuero del puerco. ¡Jajaja!"

As Mague put on her *chonis*, Felisa led the cackling, delighting in how the rodeo culminated. "How lucky can you get! You even got to use the pig's skin instead of a rock. It must have felt like using a toothbrush on your *cola*!"

On the greatest day of their life, *las sinvergüenzas* and friends *soflamaron* the story to see who could tell it best all the way home. As they had played hooky that day, they made a pact not to tell anybody. "¡Sí dices, te friego! Better not tell anybody, or else," Felisa ordered. And they kept the secret until that first Thanksgiving. Amá laughed at the story, despite being the last to know. She laughed as she had in México.

Mague was the first Tejana in Tabasco to break a pig and live to talk about it!

Without the monster in our midst, we could now live life and have fun even from our bad luck or at our own expense.

Say It Loud

Moni, short for *muñeca*, because she was as pretty as a doll, came into my life soon after Father was removed. Sharing broken families and music, we loved the Beatles and the L.A. style with its mod-Chicano music of the Midnighters, Cannibal and the Headhunters, and the Premiers. We knew their songs by heart. Felisa could always make us cry with "The Town I Live In," by the Midnighters.

> Town I live in is sad and lonely
> It's so lonely I could die.

Moni's favorite Beatle was John because he was into dope and revolution. Mague liked George because he was the tender and quiet one. Felisa was crazy over cute Paul and cared only about his looks. I liked Ringo because he was ugly and nobody else liked him. We never fought over which Beatle we liked. There were enough to go around for the four of us.

My best friend was not the clean-cut, surfer-girl type in our school— she was a mod *chuca*, a girl gangster wearing short skirts, turtlenecks, and net stockings with Mary Jane shoes. Ratted-up bouffant so stiff with Aqua Net, every hair in the front was in place, but not the back, because she already looked *outasite*. Only thing that mattered was the front. Didn't have to tend to the back, which looked like birds could nest there for a season. Her large eyes wore painted-on bottom lashes à la Twiggy.

Made her look like Orphan Annie. Pearly white lipstick made her lips fuller.

We met in the quad of old Santa Clara High School. That was where all the lost souls and troublemakers gathered. Moni asked me, "Where do we eat lunch?"

"You're here, *zonsa*," dummy, I thought, walking her to the burger pit.

Thrived on L.A. dances. Our favorite one was the jerk. Moni helped me perfect the James Brown, previously known as the mashed potatoes. And that was just the beginning.

In demand, we never sat out a dance. Some boys followed us like groupies into the various dance halls—the Whatzit, the "Y," and the Continental crowds liked to see us coming because that meant more boys were trailing behind us.

When we learned to appreciate Mexican music, the same thing happened. But we had to learn to stick out our butts because *cochinos* at the Rainbow, Balconades, or the Starlight wanted to cop a feel. Listening to Little Joe, Latin Breed, Ruben Ramos, and other groups made us real Chicanas.

For the concert of my life, I had raised money from a dance we girls had thrown with Jimmy and the Barons of Soul. Moni, my sisters, and I had worked picking prunes in the summer to pay the band. We rented the Portuguese IDES Hall. Ronnie Hall, who owned two soul record stores in town, sponsored us. We charged enough to get our school clothes for the year and had money left over to spend on concerts and dances and were often found at the Continental on Friday, Saturday, and Sunday, too, and any night there was a special dance. Plus we continued to baby-sit, pick prunes, pick walnuts, and cut apricots. I sewed dresses and prepared income taxes for Mr. Vega; I used this money to buy a '57 Chevy and to pay the insurance. Designed two wedding trousseaus for friends and two sets of formals for *quinceañeras*, including fifteen formals and five *madrinas* each. I was able to get my sisters and me free fabric to be in *quinceañeras* without spending the money.

The best night was the night we met James Brown at the fairgrounds.

We planned the whole thing, staying behind in the parking lot beyond closing. We conned the cops into thinking the car was broken, but we had rigged it. Told them someone was coming to take us home. But we lied. Wanted to meet James Brown and the Flames.

I knew how to pull the sparkplug wires out so that my gang of six girls and three boys could execute the plan. Steve and Richard wanted to bail out right away. Floyd, the black member in our group, was with us. Put the pressure on the boys to stay with it. All for one and one for all, we squeezed in between the horizontal bars of the entry gates that led to the grounds. The girls, in our best wide-leg bell-bottoms, with matching vests and rumba-sleeved blouses, slithered in with little problem. As the skinniest one of all, Moni went first. She dove in with her head carefully turned to the side, didn't want to mess her hair. As each one took their turn, some of us had to pull and push where a hip or a *chichi* got stuck. Boys were chickening out after sneaking in already. Bunch of sissies, didn't know how to have fun. We teased them so much they had no choice.

The nine of us, hiding among the bushes and watching out for the guards, walked the long way to the concert hall. We scurried up the stairs to the dressing room. Climbing up, I felt high with anticipation, trying to be silent. I was sure that our heartbeats would give us away. In front of the dressing room, Felisa and Moni knocked. I thought I would die! Didn't want to be arrested, but we had gone too far to leave now. Knock! Knock! Knock!

One of the Flames, don't know which one, greeted us, still decked out in his "Please, Please, Please" lamé cape. That was our favorite song, next to "Say It Loud. I'm Black and I'm Proud."

Didn't wait to get invited inside. Moni and Felisa left the rest of us behind. The chicken boys, Richard, Steve, and Floyd, had ditched us somewhere as we came to the dressing room. Didn't want to be perceived as fools. Missed the story of their lives. Even Floyd, who was black and proud, didn't have enough guts to stick around with us.

Some of the musicians tried to throw us out of the dressing room. But then James Brown appeared. Stopped them dead in their tracks, laughing at our moxie. Moni and my sister Felisa lunged at him like magnets and slurped him up in their arms. He responded with a sweet kiss to their cheeks, while the rest of us huddled inside in a ball of disbelief. My best friend and Felisa swore they would never wash their faces again.

With Moni around, my sisters and I had a true friend. She made it easy to forget the pain.

She kept her head in a

jar by the door

Mantuvo su cabeza en el

jarrón junto a la puerta

Surviving without a Father

Pelliscos kept us in line. Pinches reminded us to behave. Amá used them only when no other approach worked. But she never hurt us or beat us.

She loved us and took care of us. For the first time there were no limits. We could dress how we wanted, as long as our clothes met her code of decency—miniskirts not too short and see-through blouses only with camisoles. The food she bought was for everyone. Special treats no longer had to be hidden for our father to savor in our presence while we salivated with yearning. We had friends, and they could spend the night. We still had restrictions about staying at somebody else's house, though. She had a reason not to trust.

"If you couldn't trust your father, how can I trust strangers?"

As a family we began to dance around love. We learned to tell each other that we mattered. Touching and kissing were the first steps. For once it felt right.

Mother learned to tell us she loved us with touch, words, and special messages. Cooked our favorite meals and gave us money for cafeteria treats, money that she saved with much sacrifice. So we could belong. She claimed to have no favorites. She loved us all equally. Still, she thought her boys needed to be loved a bit more. She must have wanted to protect them from our father's evil example. Didn't want them to be like him. Through them she wanted to cleanse his sins.

Mother was the emotional and financial anchor of the family. No one would have predicted it. Alejandrina Barrón de Méndez, who barely spoke English, never learned to drive, and was completely dependent on my father. She became a single parent of nine at the age of thirty-five.

"El gobierno me quitó el marido. No voy a trabajar hasta que María cresca."

Insisting that the government took her husband, Amá did not work until María was of age to go to school. She kept her word. Because she held the government accountable for taking Father away, she didn't feel any guilt for staying home. It wasn't as if she wanted to take advantage; she just wanted the option to take care of us. Make sure we turned out okay.

Amá worked miracles with the limited amount of money she received from welfare to support a family of ten, including Juan Carlos. She was so good with money that she always could bail someone out of an emergency.

When she bought groceries, she purchased things by bulk before it was in style. We ate ground beef once or twice a week—she could make one pound stretch to feed ten mouths by adding potatoes, green beans, *verdolagas, nopales,* or other vegetables. She put Hamburger Helper to shame. Chicken was a treat. Our fish diet was limited to the dried shrimp patties we ate during Lent, mixing them with eggs to go a long way. She found a way to buy us fruit and cookies, something Father had bought only for himself.

No one would have suspected we were a poor family on welfare. We didn't lack anything.

Amá was thankful to have the support. Didn't have to put up with my father's crap. The state needed only a monthly report, and no abuse came with its support. We ate and were clothed no differently from before. Made do with what we had. It was better than living in the inferno my father created. No longer his chattel property, we were given choices through welfare assistance. But for the stares of other grocery shoppers when Amá and I went to the market, no one would have known we were public charges.

Even though I felt like disappearing into the shelves when she used food stamps to pay for our food at the register, Amá held her head up high.

"Es dinero."

It was money to her. Didn't matter that it came in different colors— orange, blue, pink, and purple. It still paid for the food we ate. Coupons were as good as cash. Amá figured out how to save money for those items that were not allowed, like toilet paper, soap, detergent, toothpaste, and the Kotex the four of us needed for our monthly visit.

At the Pink Elephant Market where we regularly shopped, Don Manuel, who tended the vegetables, often came to bag our groceries. It wasn't his job, but I think he liked Amá.

He greeted us with a smile as big as the ears of corn he tended, and he treated us no differently from shoppers who paid with cash. He almost sang my mother's name when he called it.

"Good morning, Mrs. Méndez."

"Gud morrnin," Amá managed back, eyes cast down to avoid his appreciation of her. Feigning to move about the store to find something or other, he would bump into her again. "Cara, Alexandrina," his English was soft and with a Spanish accent, but it might have been from Italy.

With my jealous seventeen-year-old eyes, I saw the gleam. I could guess what his interest was.

"Viejo volado," I muttered under my breath. Wanted her to know I had noticed. Although Don Manuel had a resemblance to a bald Marcello Mastroianni, only Pedro Infante could have awakened my mother's interest in men. At one time he had been my fantasy father.

She could have cared less about Don Manuel. Embarrassed. She wasn't interested. She was married for life. And that was that. Didn't matter that he was a good-for-nothing because the Catholic Church blessed her matrimony, making it "until death do you part, *hasta que la muerte los separe.*" She bought that. She believed in God.

With my help as the oldest and my '57 Chevy, Amá kept doctors' appointments, made school meetings, and wrote her welfare reports. Always on time, she kept her commitments.

As soon as she could, Amá enrolled in night school to learn English. She wanted to help my brothers and sisters with their schoolwork. After learning to speak English better, she enrolled in adult education classes and took math and other courses. Staying in school allowed her to meet the welfare's expectation of doing something with her time, even though she had more than enough keeping her busy with her enormous brood. It wasn't easy to go it alone. Wanting to continue her education and out of conviction that we would be better off with her at home, Amá remained a stay-at-home mom. Although she constantly struggled with the welfare department's push to send her off to work, she stayed home until Mary was seven years old. That was the welfare's limit for allowing my mother to remain at home.

When she could no longer stay, Amá sought the help of Comadre Sofia Eros. Her boyfriend, Simón, hired Amá to work in the fields. Later on, Anita Muñoz, who was from San Antonio, helped her to get a job as a kitchen helper in the school district. That was the beginning of her career as a food service worker.

Amá always made sure she found jobs that let her be home before her children. This meant she had to get up at 2:30 a.m. She left food ready for us. She made lunches for the younger ones or left money for the cafeteria. She didn't expect us to be the mother substitutes, as we had with Father, but we helped her when we could. Our job was to be students and to do our best.

We grew with each other, with her guidance. She became her own person and taught us to have hope. Helped us not to dwell on the past. She allowed us to make friends, opening our home to those of whom she approved. This way, she could keep an eye on things.

Ganga de Santa Clara

In our neighborhood there weren't any Chicanos who embraced their identity with all that was good about the United States and México. Joe Mendiola, a Mexican American from Texas, was as close as we had to one. He was a biker who liked to sling a few words of Tex-Mex Spanish here and there. Tried to impress us with his *caló*. "¡Esas! Esos vatos." Words spiced his hamburger-patty English as he used *rucas* and *wisas* to refer to us girls. Made us laugh at him, rather than think him the Chicano man-about-town that he thought he was.

It was not unusual for us to drive eighteen miles each way, from Santa Clara to San José, to see *raza*, our people, and to meet boys. We could have taken Highway 101 to get there, but it was boring. Nothing to see on the freeway, so we took city streets, beginning with El Camino Real, which turned into The Alameda, which became Santa Clara, and finally Alum Rock Avenue to King Road. Living in a white town, we traveled the *barrio* streets to see Chicanos because there were none in Santa Clara.

In 1966 we ventured out in the coolest and most souped-up Chevy you've ever seen to those places that would have been off limits. Gloria, Jane, Wendi, Diane, Amy, Becky, Hermie, Felisa, Moni, Olga, and Susie were the only Chicana friends we had in high school. Back in those days hardly anyone admitted to being Mexican. The only one was Mike Mendoza, the darkest of us all, who chased surfer girls with long, blond tresses, ignoring *las indias*. There were no boys to our liking; therefore, we went to find them in the streets of San José.

Cruising, we were tagged by the boys as "the Santa Clara gang." I was made the leader. We weren't really a *clica*, just a bunch of *chavas* mostly concerned with going to dances and concerts. We all dressed alike. Decked out in our black vests, bell-bottom pants with the widest of legs, and long-sleeved blouses, we stood out. Of course we looked good; I designed and sewed the outfits we wore.

Because I was shy and didn't go after boys, I became the ideal *jefa* for the *ganga*. They listened to me, and I was in charge. I had only two rules: We came home on time, and we returned together. No exceptions!

"You have to come back with us, otherwise you'll never hang out with us again," I laid down the law to la Twiggy, Wendy, and the other groupies. *Mensas* didn't seem to learn.

"If you ditch us, don't ever expect to hang out with us again." And I meant it.

A white, surfer high school with upper-class wannabes, Santa Clara was packed with Portuguese and Italian *gringos*. Filipinos, who spoke Tagalog and Iloqano, and a few lost Mexicans, who spoke only English, gave the school what little color it had. But it didn't have boys we liked. Too white, too blond, and too dorky—that's how we saw them. Found nothing attractive or interesting about them or their culture. Except for la Wendi Jiustón, whose last name wasn't a Mexican town but a Texas city, Houston, who changed her name to *español* because she wanted to be Mexican. She tailed after us so-called chongs, a *gringo* word for *pachucas*, to have a good time. She told us that her pilot father didn't want her to act so Mexican since she looked white. La Wendi desperately wanted to have the dark looks and hair of her Mexican mother, who acted *gringa*.

The surfer boys of our youth liked the wrong music, wore the wrong clothes, and couldn't dance if bullets were sprayed in their direction. Besides, they would have wanted us for only one thing because they saw Mexicans as chili hot and ready to give it up for the asking. That's why we went after Chicanos, guys who waited to ask before they jumped our bones.

To my surprise, Richard caught me. He was from Sal Si Puedes. He was a little *gordo* but cuddly. A *güero* with a handsome face, he didn't wear the starched Levis that stood up or the leather jacket that we admired so. He dressed like a *mojado* in the plaid shirt, surfer style of the day.

"He's a dork," *la ganga* disapproved. Made fun of me because they wanted the bad boys to like us. They were more exciting, and Richard was too good to be true, until he tried to put his hand inside my blouse. *¡Cabrón!* Who did he think he was?

Got the slap of his young life. "I'm not that kind of girl. If that's what you're looking for, we're through. *¡Pendejo!*"

Never saw Richard again. *Cabrón.* He was like all the rest.

We *chucas* kept on cruising, as we hunted San José's main drag and made friends with dangerous and daring boys who liked us because we were *locas* enough to go searching for them. Had no trouble finding *novios.*

With a chrome record player that played 45s mounted on the dash of my Chevy, we'd roll the oldies of the day and the soul sounds of Motown, howling as cute guys passed.

> *Ahooooooo!* You sure are looking good!
> You're everythin' that a big bad wolf could want. *Ahooooooo!*

Felisa was even better than the great Wolfman Jack, the Number One DJ. And we showed those girls we could take their boys away from them when we wanted. Let them know they had something to worry about and that the boys were there for the taking. They thought we were badass, and we acted the part.

We, the Santa Clara gang, were hot, and we knew it. No one would have guessed I was just baby-sitting my two younger sisters, and they were pulling the strings. I was just there for the trip.

Looks, Body, and Mind

Every chance they had, our friends and neighbors told my mother the truth: Margaret had the looks; Felisa had the body; and I was the thinker. What they meant to say was that I was ugly, but smart. I could read it in their eyes. And I think I agreed with them.

Amá would listen patiently and say nothing, although inside she was seething. She loved us equally and didn't favor one over the other. Even though we sisters had always heard our relatives say that they preferred light complexions, Amá had long learned that color didn't matter when you worked in the field.

I pretended their comments didn't bother me. But they did.

When I looked at myself in the mirror, I saw a *cara de caballo*, a long horse-face kid, with fat cheeks and small *chinche* eyes. I could never find anything attractive about myself, no matter how hard I looked.

My looks were pieces of a puzzle that didn't fit, something I had to put together.

I resented the attention that Mague received. Although she was short, her features were European. Small-breasted, she looked like a waif in a Dickens novel. Wore hot pants to show off her skinny legs and cupcake ass so that a piece of *nalga* would protrude. She always had gobs of eyeliner for her Batman eyes. Never let us see her without her face on, and she slept in her false eyelashes. Woke up with them sometimes pasted on her cheeks.

I envied Felisa's looks. She had a nineteen-inch waist with wide hips and boobs to match their width, like a real-life Playboy Bunny sticker. Made women especially jealous. Hated to see her coming. She was so beautiful that even the *gringas* hated her for looking like them, only better. Felisa's long, chestnut hair proved that not all Mexicans ironed their curly hair.

Everyone noticed my sisters. Ignored me.

But my smarts made up for their looks, I repeated over and over, burying my nose in the books. I had that; my sisters didn't.

My dancing made me popular because I could move to the beat of any sound. Gave the *ganga* a run for their money as the boys asked *me* to dance. On the dance floor looks didn't matter. Rhythm did. Danced with anyone who asked, but I had my limits. Toads were just fine for me. *Pero la ganga* was too picky and sat out more songs than I care to count. Didn't mind getting their rejects. *Gordos, flacos,* or pimply-faced. Drew the line at those who were too *pedos* to dance, too drunk to do the moves. I didn't want to waste my talent on them. I also said no to those who wanted to *meter pierna,* who got too close. Tried to rub their boner against me and attempted to stick either leg between mine. Didn't let them. Danced with my butt up in the air, a hissing *pinacate* that withdraws from an attack. This beetle bug still managed all the steps.

On the dance floor my brain didn't get in the way of my dancing. Being smart wasn't enough, though. Being ugly was painful.

It wasn't until I found the images of Mexican Indian women that I began to appreciate myself. Women in the Mexican calendars were comic-book mirrors of me, yet they were often making *tortillas* or swooning on the arms of warriors. Chavela and the Brown Express, a Chicana singer who played at the Tropicana, and *india*-looking activists in San José gave me the alternatives I sought. Because of them I accepted my looks.

With him gone, I could now find my beauty. *Los labios gruesos* that I tried to stretch into the perfectly thin Anglo smile became full once again. Started wearing lipstick on my "nigger lips." Laughed without covering my mouth. Away from the *gringo* surfer standards and my father's taunting, I reclaimed my looks. Paint on my face made me visible. Lipstick the color of mother-of-pearl white that made my lips more luscious, daringly becoming the *más trompuda.*

My *mestiza* roots and my brown color were next, something I was expected to tone down. My Indianness came in handy when the Chicanos came out of the woodwork, discovering our Indian heritage. Having gone to school in México, I knew my roots. Never lost my Spanish, although my Indian tongue was gone in the First Conquest. Funny, some Chicanos even began to sprinkle around the Spanish words they had denied me since elementary school. Tiki Soares and Bertha Gomes came out as Chicanos.

Small nose, high cheekbones, slanted eyes. *Chata. India. China.* Nicknames I accepted with pride. But I had a hard time with the hair on my upper lip.

Women in my mother's family all have the famous Barrón mustache. Guess it came from their French grandfather or Italian grandmother. My female relatives were hairy women who never even imagined shaving their legs or underarms. For them hair was natural and proof of their European lineage. Made nothing of it. All my *tías* laughed at the jokes about being *bigotonas.* In the United States not having hair was a good thing, but being an *india* wasn't.

For me a hairy lip was a disaster. Kids made fun of me and called me Emiliano Zapata, Francísco Villa, and sometimes Cantinflas. When being nice, boys called me Doña *Josefa* Ortiz de Dominguez, a co-conspirator of the Mexican War of Independence from Spain, because she had a mustache, too.

I was involved in many fights over those *bigotes.* I'll never forget *los disparates,* their jokes and their teasing. But deep inside I took pride in my membership in the Mexican Legion of Honor. I was in good company.

Piece by piece, my lips, eyes, skin color, and even my mustache made me whole. I could see myself in the mirror and look beyond the shame.

On Not Becoming *Putas*

We abused girls who survived were drawn to each other like fireflies to light. Our lonely hearts and mangled souls made us friends. We, discarded and brokenhearted girls, were attracted to each other like magnets. We created the embrace we needed to feel; we helped each other to survive.

Don't know how. But we could always tell. Felt it in our skin.

When we weren't sure about our history of abuse, Amy and Becky in their drunken stupor or on a high spilled their secrets. Became brave enough to let out the pain. Confessions cleansed spirits. Jane and Diane cowered behind the sadness, praying not to be discovered. Together in silence, we girls created a sisterhood of survival.

Still, we had our problems. Hermie shoplifted. Some were attracted only to bad-assed Chicanos. Wendi drank too much and allowed every Juan, José, and Fernando to paw her because she wasn't into Toms, Harrys, or Dicks.

"Good thing we're here. *Si no*, they'd all get a piece." Watching out for her, any one of us girls could chime the warning bell of caution.

Jane, who always wanted to be a Smith instead of a López, ballooned. Paid no mind to her size. Claimed she came from big-boned Spaniards. Said she was comfortable in her belly, claiming her *lonja* power.

Becky stole Boone's Farm and Ripple wines, anything to soothe the pain. When it was no longer bearable, she ran, ran away to come back to beatings and isolation. Kept at home under lock and key. "Until she straightens out." Her younger sister would tattle when we went to look for her.

Gracie fell in love as often as she changed *chonis*. Freely made out and disappeared with her date of the minute into the night. Found it anywhere she could. She confused sex with love. Older sister Lina could do nothing to stop her. Gracie knew how to stray and enjoyed the attention she won.

This was the legacy of our hurt. Forever struggling with the pain, we lived life on the edge. Because she was so cute, Gracie could always get away with anything. Wendi still earned a reputation as loose, and the rest of us were never called easy. *Moscamuerta* Gracie seemed too innocent to do anything bad, and the boys never told when she did because rewards came with silence. Some people are like busy flies that are easily flattened by a swatter. Then there are those flies that pretend they're already dead and get away, like Gracie.

We friends looked after each other. As the oldest, I found myself often looking behind the bushes. Made sure black beauties, yellow jackets, or other pills didn't fall into their hands. Stopped them from drinking too much. But couldn't protect them from the smoke-highs of maryjane. Had some stay overnight when they were too polluted to go home. Cleaned up vomit. Loaned them clothes to get home the next day. Made excuses. Gave them alibis. Kept them out of the group when it happened more than once.

Mague, Felisa, and I did not become *putas*. Those who knew about us wondered.

Afraid of older men, we stayed away. Suspected Compadre Sancho and avoided him. However, we didn't fear boys our own age. They were different. Didn't associate violence with them. Boys were aliens to me. After the slapping incident with my first boyfriend, Richard, I didn't care to have them around except in friendship. I thought some were cute, but that was it. I let my friends explore, and I lived through their adventures.

I learned from their experiences, until I met Paco. Suave and good-looking, who could dance up a storm, he grew closer than most. Didn't want what happened with my father to happen with him. Sloppy kissing and groping my breasts were as far as he went. When he tried to go further, I gave him a better slap than the one I gave Richard. Embarrassed that I slapped him, I scurried when I saw him at the Rainbow Ballroom.

Romance. Who had time for it? I just wanted to be a girl, dealing with puppy love from afar. Didn't want to deal with sex.

Because Amá stayed home, we turned out fine. With her around and my father gone, we could be young girls. She let us go out with friends. For the first time boys could call us, even if for only three to five minutes.

Felisa, of course, figured out how to get more time. To get more boy-friends and telephone time, she went by different names, some of which were Yolanda, Yesenia, Yasmin, Happy, and Esperanza; this way her minutes stretched into hours. It also kept her from committing to one boy. Gave her anonymity. She wanted to have fun, but that was all. Never gave out our address, but she handed out our telephone number left and right. Don't know how she kept up, but she did. Felisa matched her aliases and personality with the boys she attracted. Any serious contenders had to meet Amá if they wanted to visit.

Amá let us be. She did not intrude.

She let boys come into our lives. She allowed them to be around us.

We didn't have to hide. Welcomed and made them at home. Appreciated some to the point of including them in the family. Made them flour *tortillas* and fed them. We could see Amá trusted our choice of friends. But our girlfriends didn't have Amá. They had to search for who they were in other ways. With her in our lives, we did not become the bad girls we pretended to be.

Still, sexuality was confusing. I wanted nothing to do with it. Margaret found that she could use her body to get a real boyfriend because she didn't want to stay a lonely teenage mother. Felisa had no trouble dodging and trapping the many who swarmed her way. She discarded them as if they were fashions that went out of style, changing them with the seasons or when they didn't match.

Raised inside the boundaries of virginity and the demands of our father's brutality, we were scared of sex. We saw it as a sin. Believed it to be something done only when blessed by the sacrament of marriage. However, we felt branded by our father's sins. Trapped by the shame and still blaming ourselves for what happened, it was difficult to contend with sex. For my sisters and me, sex was a mixture of violence and betrayal. Mague, on the other hand, took risks, attempting to find love in it somewhere.

Still, we figured it out. Felisa and I wouldn't take chances being alone with boys. Group dating kept us away from the pressures of sex. Took us out of situations that would have compromised us. Kept us safe, hanging out with boys our own age.

We started to become the women we wanted to be. We were not our father's whores.

Yellow Dress and Graduations

Made my own dress for high school graduation. It had been two brief years after father's incarceration and the colors in my life were coming back. My dress was bright yellow and orange with greens, with huge red hibiscus flowers that dominated the nylon print, lined with yellow satin. I wore deep yellow, square-toed shoes to complement that tent dress that Mama Cass was famous for wearing. Mother and all my brothers and sisters came, arriving late like a mama duck trailed by her *patitos*. They sat all in a row, beaming with pride to see their oldest sister, the first to graduate, receive her diploma. Didn't have a party, but my family feasted on Amá's world-famous chicken *mole*, rice, and beans with homemade flour *tortillas*. Didn't have a cake. My nineteen-year-old accomplishment, after having spent three years in the sixth grade thanks to my father's moving around, didn't take away from their pride.

I had always wanted to go to college, but Santa Clara University was a private Catholic institution that did not consider people like me who didn't have the money or the status to be there. Instead, I went to West Valley, a local community college filled with slackers who would rather be surfing in Santa Cruz. I had no choice but to study business because I had been prepared to be a bilingual secretary. Only lasted a semester. I was lucky not to flunk out of all my classes because I was so bored.

After dropping out of West Valley because I felt invisible as one of the few Mexicans, I went to work.

Still at home, I took my dancing feet to Arthur Murray's. I lasted only a morning. The trouble began when I questioned their policy of not soliciting businesses with the prefixes that began with 251, 258, and 259—all known to be Mexican phone numbers on the other side of the tracks. I told them to eat their paycheck, and I walked away. Next, I went to work as an operator for the telephone company. Amá never expected me to give her my paycheck. Shared it only when I wanted to, unlike the days when we had no choice with my father.

Mague then graduated from high school and went to a beauty college. She found an apartment and moved in with her son. Felisa, still in high school, was carrying on a romance with a guy I didn't like. Too much like my father. He had the same mad look in his eyes, but she married him before graduation.

Unmasking the Monster

Released early for good behavior, my father did only three years in prison before he came sniffing around Amá.

We found out that he was courting her again, behind our backs. Bet he came around with a million reasons why we needed him. Must have wanted to raise his sons. Told Mother what she wanted to hear.

He waited around another three years after his release, hoping to talk Amá into taking him back. Used baby Mary, now six years old, as his lure. Mary's desire for a father's love added to Amá's pressure to take him back. She didn't know better.

"Prison has made me a different man. I've paid for what I've done. Alejandrina, take me back. You won't regret it. I'll make it up to you, Alejandrina. After all, your daughters are grown. They don't need me. But you and my boys do. Nunca he dejado de quererte."

I still lived with the fear of his return. I suspected my mother's husband, which is how I thought of my father now, would come back to harm my baby sisters. Sonia and María had been spared. And we three older sisters would stop him at any cost. I would not hesitate to kill him this time.

Mague, Felisa, and I had no evidence, but we knew he would return.

One Sunday, when she was already married to someone who was too much like my father, Felisa dropped by Amá's. Coincidentally, she arrived at the same time as two cousins we hadn't seen since we left Tabasco. They were related to us through Father.

Stepping out of the car to greet them, Felisa noticed that Father was also inside their car. Confused, she excused herself and ran into the house.

Once inside she vomited. Distressed and cussing up a storm, she demanded to know what the hell he was doing there. Mother did not yet know that he was outside.

Felisa told Mother to get rid of him.

"Who the fuck does he think he is? What gave him the right to be here? *Pinche viejo*, get him the hell out!"

Terrified by his presence, Felisa stayed inside the house until my mother chased him away. Felisa couldn't believe Amá would allow him to come around the house.

Later, Felisa told Mague, who didn't waste any time confronting Mother. Mague rushed to Amá's and threatened to take the younger kids away from her. Told Amá she would go to the authorities if she even contemplated allowing him in the house ever again.

"I'll never let my little sisters suffer the way we did. It's your business if you want to get back with him. But you'll have to do that alone. As long as I'm alive, you'll never go back to him. Not with the children, you will not. I'll take you to court if I have to," Mague daringly told our mother. Her threats must have convinced Amá to put an end to his visits. That was the last time anyone saw him or heard about his presence around the house.

To her credit, Amá got rid of him this time. That was the end of her romance.

Baby Mary was barely fourteen when I told her everything. Having banished her idealized father from the picture, I was the one she hated.

I sat with her. Gave her the reasons for the breakup of our family. Told her that he wasn't the father she thought he was. He was an evil man who hurt her older sisters. Besides beating us, he touched and hurt us in ways no father should hurt his daughters. I didn't want him to do that to Mary. He went to prison for it. I didn't want him to hurt Mary, too. She was better off without a father. Forget him, I told her. I didn't want her to end up his victim.

I destroyed the father of Mary's dreams, exposing him for what he was. Her innocence killed, she never mentioned him again. We also stopped his advances on our mother and finally let my younger sisters know about the man who was their father. Like old times, I knew that I would be the target of his rage.

 ## Corazones y coraje

He had promised to kill me when he was released.

After all, he credited me for unleashing the secrets that sent him to prison. But he gave me too much credit. As strong as I was, I lived in fear of him like the rest of the family. I continued to hope he would stay away from us.

A few years later, Tío Mayo called to let us know that Father had suffered a heart attack. Already twenty-two, I felt like a scared child again. Yet, I felt the obligation to call him. But I stopped myself. Then I dialed his number, hoping to reach him before he died. I hung up again. Had buried him long ago.

I wanted him dead. If he died, then he would be out of my life. I didn't feel compassion for him, but I was confused. We would be better off without him in the world. Still, I also felt pity, though the pity didn't keep me from wishing him the most gruesome of deaths. Thinking I wouldn't be able to confront him if he died, I felt enraged. I wanted my day in court and for him to know how I felt about his betrayal. I dialed again. He picked up the phone—too late to hang up. The phone shook in my hands as I heard his voice.

Bién educada, the compulsory greeting I had been taught slid from my mouth before I could stop it. Spoke to him in the language of compliance and obedience.

"Buenos días, es Josefina. ¿Cómo se siente? How do you feel? How's your heart?"

It took a heart attack for me to realize he had a heart after all. Anxious, I felt stuck between laughter and tears. Didn't know what to do. I spoke English to him, attempting to create a sense of distance. I wanted to be in control. Didn't give him a chance to answer.

I blurted what I had been holding inside for so long, words tripping from my tongue with the desire to let him know all I had harbored inside. The words kept coming.

"Tío Mayo called to tell me you had a heart attack. I hate you for all the pain you caused our family. I'm still angry with you. I'm still trying to get rid of the hate I have for you, but it hasn't been easy. I'm trying to put the past behind. But I don't fear you anymore. *¡Pobre Viejo!* I don't think you have the guts to kill me. But I have them for both of us. I forgive you."

My words must have surprised him. I was the last person from whom he wanted to hear.

Don't remember what he said, but that call gave me back my dignity. Shed the fear once and for all.

The hate would take more time.

As he faced his mortality, I had forced him to confront his sins. Long hoodwinked into thinking my sisters and I had seduced him, his family finally learned our side of the story. It would be clear that I had called *para reprocharle el pasado*, to rebuke him for the past, and to remind him of the pain he had caused us. Alejandrina had raised her daughters well, after all.

"¡Qué Dios lo perdone! May God forgive you!" And He must have, because God kept him on this earth. My father survived the heart attack.

Having been taught to forgive, especially when somebody is near death, I made an effort to forgive him, but I was really trying to forgive myself. As easy as it may sound, it was one of the most difficult things I have had to do in my life. The confrontation gave me a sense of person-hood. No more a *chingada vieja*, I was a loving and good woman.

To uncover Amá's role in our pain, I would have to go to her to fill in the gaps, not an easy task.

Pláticas con mi madre

I didn't know where to begin. I never imagined how stressful it would be to discuss the topic with her, to ask Amá about his betrayal. Where to begin? But talk we did.

Heading southeast toward Stockton one cold December morning to visit Amá's family, I finally had my chance. I was afraid to open up the wounds. I started out with questions that sounded gentle and didn't judge her because I knew she then would not talk. I didn't want her to recoil inside the shame; therefore, I attempted not to cast blame. I felt like crying at her answers, but I stopped myself. I knew how to do that well. Once I asked the first question, the rest seemed to be louder and harsher. She listened and tried to answer.

¿Qué usted no sabía lo que pasaba?

¿Qué no veía lo que él hacía?

¿Porqué lo ignoró?

¿A poco usted no sabía lo que el hacía?

¿Cómo que no lo creía?

How could you not know?

How could you not feel?

How could you not see? How is it possible not to see?

Why did you let him get away with it?

Why didn't you stop him?

Protect us. Stop him. Trap him. See him. Don't let him get away.

Stop him. Stop him. Stop him.

Spoke English to her, my language of liberation and the tongue that gave me freedom from his grasp. Repeated every word to make sure she understood. Didn't know how else to do it. Wanted her to answer.

In a torrent of tears and Spanish, Amá answered.

"Yosi. Yo no me imaginaba que tu padre fuera tan vil. Esto nunca pasó en mi familia, y no me permitía creer que algo así pasara. A veces, cuando sospechaba de él, lo interrogaba. ¡Tu padre me acusaba de loca!"

Amá couldn't imagine a father would be so cruel. She never had one to compare him with, and none of her brothers would have ever hurt their baby sister in the way he hurt his own daughters. Nothing like this had ever happened in her family. She had no choice but to believe his lies.

Alone and isolated, she relied on him for everything. She had no choice. In a foreign land, unable to protest her treatment, having married him at fifteen, she knew no other way. Tied to him, she could see no options.

There were times she allowed herself to suspect a truth so horrible, but she put it out of her mind. She had no place to go. No one was there to help her. The fear dominated her.

She was alone with her children. She had no other means of support. She didn't see it. She didn't know that in this country you have the right to be protected against abuse. In her family such treatment wouldn't have been permitted. That's why he took her away from them.

There were times she trusted her intuition and confronted him. He made her believe she was crazy. How could a mother who loved her daughters have such evil and filthy thoughts about her daughters and their own father?

He told her she was sick.

He taunted her about being jealous. Made her feel vile and used her intuition against her, prevented her from protecting us.

"¿Cómo puedes pensar así de mi? Soy bueno contigo. Soy un buen prójimo. How could you think that of me? I'm good to you. I am a Good Samaritan."

Exploiting his reputation as a good provider and husband, my father would bank on his generosity to others. He dismissed her questions.

Still feeling the sting of his mockery, ridicule, and accusations, Amá cried like the ghost of *la llorona*, still weeping for the children she lost. I stopped the conversation. Decided I had asked enough questions for one afternoon.

Amá and I ended our drive in silence. We both knew the conversation would continue. We had the rest of our lives to talk.

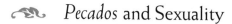 *Pecados* and Sexuality

Already a young woman, I was still fearful of sex. Didn't let myself think about it or desire it. Knew more than I cared to know about it. Sex and betrayal were the same to me. My father's touches had aroused me. I knew it was a sin. It wasn't a touch of love between a father and his daughter. I withdrew in disgust. His touch had turned possible joy into something to shun, deny, or repress. The wrong touch turned me off. But sometimes I thought about welcoming it from someone else.

My father had made it easier not to be sexual.

I swore to remain intact for marriage, as expected of a good Catholic girl. I was no floozy. I did not compromise to be popular, but I could have. Didn't want to do anything with boys that wouldn't happen in the daylight with a bunch of friends to witness. Sex and his abuse were intertwined.

I still wanted intimacy, so I let myself explore.

I started by learning to give and receive hugs, pats, and other affections from my family and friends. Little by little I figured out the difference among touches.

Kissing games let me feel sexual in a safe way. My lips could show my desire for sex, but they kept me in control of my emotions. On my terms I could savor the heat that came with passion. Without guilt.

Because of my father's betrayal, my body had not been my own. Kissing was a way to get it back. Because my father had not touched my lips, I could start there.

Sola pero mejor acompañada

Of our family life in the United States, only two formal portraits have survived: one of Father and Mother, and the other of Amá holding my brother Juan. He was about six months old when it was taken in Chicago sometime in early 1957.

In the photo of Juan and my mother, a furniture piece that looks like a piano or a fancy radio console stands in the background. It's to the right of my mother. Despite our family's love for music, we were too poor to afford a piano. It must have been a console. In that photo is another picture of my parents when they were young and in love. In the picture within the picture, Amá is wearing the outfit I remember her donning when she sang "Amorcito Corazón." This image is a snapshot in time, reminding me of that part of our family history we left behind in Tabasco with Tía Herme, reminding me of the love Mother had for him.

We did not meet my brother Juan until he was a toddler of two, when he visited Tabasco with my father. He was a terror. With his pointed cowboy boots, he liked to kick and to give us orders. A Don Chepo in training boots, Juan was beginning to copy our father's behavior, *de tal palo tal astilla.*

Inspecting the photo of Juan and my mother, I see my baby sister Mary's resemblance to Amá. Didn't look at all like Abuela Cuca, as relatives on my father's side have always claimed. Mary was a carbon copy of Amá. With shoulder-length hair and a slight body, Mother, in a virgin-like pose holding Baby Jesús, held her firstborn son, Juan. He was to have been her salvation. She finally did it right. After five *pinche viejas* she had his boy.

My father must have taken that picture. Left his mark on it, with that "Amorcito Corazón" photo of theirs. Couldn't extricate him from our lives. He was central. Unlike snapshots we tore to pieces of boyfriends and friends who had fallen from grace in our lives, we could not remove him.

Like the picture inside the picture, his violence resides within our bodies. Although gone, his memory lingers like that black-and-white photograph of our parents that we can't extricate from the picture of Amá and Juan. His memory lives in our cells.

Amá was rid of his violence, but her price was loneliness.

She chose her children over a life with men. Giving up her sensuality, she devoted herself to us. Even though she was surrounded by our love, she remained a woman alone, *una mujer sola*. Amá has accepted this as her lot in life. It was her cross to carry for falling in love with my father.

As we continued to talk, there were moments of reflection for Amá. It was during those times that she expressed regret, wishing she had known then what she knows now. She would have done things differently.

It has been during those times of deep discussion that Amá has asked us for forgiveness. If only she could go back in time, she would do it differently.

 ## M'ija, at Nineteen

I often think that having no father would have been better than having a father like him. Found myself wishing I had been made by someone else.

He never called me *m'ijita*, dearest daughter.

For him I was a *vieja*, an old hag woman-child, rather than his daughter.

Never had the intimate and loving relationship that a father has with his daughter, where everything she does counts, where all she says is cute. Never had that.

I've given up that wish. Yet, my heart still stings like a paper cut that keeps opening from the pain that lingers.

I walk around like a spirit who has returned to find the reasons for not having had love. All I have been able to find is a father who didn't love me.

I have hated him so.

Still, I seek his approval. I want his acceptance, and I hate feeling that. Yet, I can't seem to help it. All I want is for him to love me like a daughter.

There are times I choke on my resentment. I close in and go inside myself with the memories of my father. I would have loved for him to call me *m'ija*. I might have settled for that at one time.

Can't cry because of him. I wish I could. He taught me not to cry. If I cried when he abused my sisters and me, he would hit me. He would also hit me if I didn't cry. How could I have learned to express this emotion?

Because of him I don't trust men. All men remind me of him. It's his fault I fear them. I don't trust them.

There are times that I'm tired of it all. I repress his memory, so that I won't be consumed with so much hate and pain. Then there are times I pretend he doesn't affect my life—I won't call him Father. Instead, I refer to him as "your husband" when speaking to my mother, or *su padre* when talking to any of my sisters or brothers. Sometimes I also call him Mr. Méndez. This allows me to render him a stranger—someone with whom I have only a surname in common.

As the thinking oldest sister, I still try to figure things out, try to understand. I want to sort it all out, but I can't seem to get there.

Searching for forgiveness, I can't find it. It's not in me yet—can't forgive myself, him, or those who failed to listen to our call for help.

There are times I get lost in the mess of it all. I know I was born of him. Yet, I don't accept him as my father—nor do I wish to have him in my life. Still haven't figured out what to call him—or if I should even acknowledge him.

A father wouldn't have put his family through what he did. He would have loved us. I still sting; the loss feels like cactus needles that won't come out—I know the needles are there, they hurt, but I cannot remove them. The pain from his betrayal and rejection remains with me like Sisyphus pushing the boulder up the mountain with no end in sight. The boulder represents all that I have to deal with, as I attempt to climb the mountain to see what is inside myself.

The anger wells up in me, and I try to be strong. Sometimes I can. Other times I break apart.

If only he had loved me enough not to abuse me. If only he had been man enough to know the difference.

For God's sake, I was his daughter! Yet for him I was really only a *chingada muchacha*.

If only my father had called me *m'ija*. If only he had loved me enough not to hurt me.

Epilogue: Purging the Skeletons, Bone by Bone

We are "written" all over, or should I say, carved and tattooed with the sharp needles of experience. . . . Some of us are forced to acquire the ability, like a chameleon, to change color when the dangers are many and the options are few.

—Gloria Anzaldúa, "Haciendo Caras, una Entrada: An Introduction," in *Haciendo Caras: Making Face, Making Soul*

I did not consciously set out to expose the evil of manipulation, the decadence of power, and the depravity of male control over powerless women and girls. With *Las hijas de Juan* I did not intentionally go about exposing my father's contempt for women, something that seemed to come from his primordial self, as I had not been exposed to such violence among my kin. Rather, with this book I set out to reveal the social power vested in my father by a society that sanctions or, at best, ignores men's violence against women and children. His treatment of us remained hidden in a culture that still colludes with the reproduction of domestic and sexual violence that kills children's spirits and denigrates women even as it venerates them because of their gender.

Since writing *Las hijas de Juan,* I have come to see it as a self-healing project that provided me a venue for understanding the ways my socialization and cultural experience as a girl helped me deal with the violence I lived with as an individual and as a member of a collective, my family. I have come to learn that healing does not always take place in the telling, but that it is recovered in the reclaiming of survival. For my sisters and me, the healing did not rest in voicing our stories, but in recognizing and accepting that we did all we could to stay alive under the circumstances.

The reclamation of my experiences and my healing journey began in early adolescence, when I witnessed the ways society dealt with Mexican

American perpetrators and victims of incest. This was made possible through the airing of a sister-brother incest case that received extensive coverage in the local newspaper and in the informal networks of our community in San José, California. The court transcripts were ominous. I will never forget those words, words that indicted my people as a group and me personally because of the blame and responsibility I had assumed for the violence in my own home.

> Don't you know that things like this are terribly wrong? This is one of the worst crimes that a person can commit. I just get so disgusted . . . you're lower than an animal. Even animals don't do that. You are pretty low . . . you haven't got any moral principles . . . your parents won't teach you what's right or wrong . . . you're no particular good to anybody. We ought to send you out of the country— send you back to Mexico. . . . You ought to commit suicide. . . . You're lower than animals and haven't the right to live in organized society—just miserable, lousy, rotten people. . . . Maybe Hitler was right. (Honorable Gerald S. Chargin, Judge, Court Room No. 1, September 2, 1969)

When the brother-sister case came to light, it had been only four years since my family's courthouse proceedings. I found myself internalizing all I heard as if it were my own experience. This is not uncommon for survivors of trauma. Judge Chargin's judgment derided Mexicans as animalistic and without morals, and I believed myself to belong to that herd of depraved subhumans of which he spoke. Yet, the activists and leaders in our community who took positions against him gave me another perspective. Their actions allowed me to interrogate and resist the scarlet mark that Chargin so venomously stamped on my people and me. Enraged by his racism, they picketed the courthouse, calling for his resignation because of his racist and dehumanizing conclusion, until he stepped down.

Through it all I did not speak, I remained silent, hiding in the shadows, fearing that I would divulge the secret I carried within—about my family and me. Glued to every word and story about the case, I evaluated my own worth and the shame I carried through those words. In the process, however, I shed some of the self-imposed burden of responsibility and started my self-conscious lifelong journey toward healing.

Finally extricated and intimately examining my hurt to write *Las hijas de Juan*, I recognized that incest is never further away than my unconscious because I live inside its scar. Incest is a wound that never closes. It reopens every time a woman or child confronts the betrayal of violence at the hands of those who have been charged with their care and have the responsibility of loving them. Moreover, because my sisters and our mother have confirmed the recollections I have about our familial betrayal, the personal has become political, for our experiences transcend the trauma of one, to include the collective remembering of the family unit.

I put pen to paper one Santa Cruz Indian summer day in 1988, when my almost twenty-six-year-old nephew, who had been spared by the culture of silence that still pervaded our family, came to talk to me about having learned of whose rape he was the product. He had always known he was the product of violence. This was not new to him. My sisters, in their desire to protect their children from abuse, had taught them to defend themselves from incest without disclosing their own experience. Mague had told my nephew about his conception one of those times when he was old enough and again asked about his father. Listening to him, I verified his finding and reassured him that I loved him. I let him know that the circumstances of his birth never made any difference in my love for him.

Since then I continued to write, not knowing where it would take me, but contemplating questions that gnawed at me. Writing helped me to deal with my feelings, emotions, and memories, but I never saw my musings as the foundation for a book, until much later.

Without realizing it, I was engaging in a journaling self-help process of healing to come to terms with my life. Then, when I moved to San Antonio, where my social circle includes writers and artists, and aided by the distance, I became inspired by a literary culture that thrived around me. I continued writing. By the year 2000, having compiled a manuscript,

I asked my husband to read it. Moved by the content and seeing the possibility in the manuscript, he told me that I had three books in one, but that I needed to tell *the* story. He didn't have to tell me which one—we both knew the story pushing to come out was the incest story.

Not ready to accept his conclusion, I continued working on the manuscript. Then, when Barbara Renaud Gonzalez, under the counsel of Sandra Cisneros, said the same thing, I finally listened. They commented that some of the stories were too superficial and, at best, runways to a story. And even though their feedback came with warnings that I would have to go deep inside myself, because of their literary authority I finally accepted that the book I was writing was about incest.

They were right. It took two years to finally get the story out. Guided by girlfriends and kindred spirits—Gloria, Barbara, Sandra, Lillie—and my husband, I finished.

But finishing wasn't as easy as it seems. That year, 2001, was my year of darkness. Along with digging inside myself, I extracted the depth of our story from my sisters and our mother. Although I had long been the spectator and protector of my mother's beatings, for the first time in my life I learned about the desecration and the insidious violence my little sisters endured. Preferring to see Mague's pregnancy as an immaculate conception, I had not let myself imagine the extent of their damage. Limiting my understanding to my own experience—inappropriate touch had been where it all began—I found out from Felisa that rape was both her and Mague's reality. Because we had never talked to each other, I had no clue, and if I had intuited it, I did not allow myself to see. Under the shadow of death—it could be Amá's or any one of us he threatened to kill—with which Juan controlled our environment, our father reinforced our family's denial. The climate under which we lived made us unable to see. He kept us in denial about our own hurt, and incapable of hearing each other's pain, blind and speechless about the horrors we lived. Speaking out was out of the question. The one coded call for help was the naming of Juan Carlos. Otherwise, the grim terror of impending death silenced us. Then, when all was made public, we sheltered ourselves in denial to protect each other from the stigma, the guilt, and the responsibility we assigned ourselves for our own victimization. We sisters did not speak about *it* to anyone—not even to ourselves. It took writing this book and speaking out to finally piece the story together.

Numbed and shocked by Felisa's disclosure, I felt and acted like a wailing *llorona,* seeking to make sense of it all. Living in tears and anger, I wrote and cried. Cried some more. For that one year I called Felisa in the wee hours of the morning to talk, to confirm stories, to ask her questions. I grieved the loss of our innocence and my inability to see or to protect my sisters. I tried to talk to Mague, but she would speak to me only about what she witnessed, not what she experienced. She had put it behind her and she wanted to keep it there, buried in the past, where it belonged. However, in her willingness to be a sounding board or my memory filler, Mague also read the manuscript in progress. She wanted to help me remember: "help you heal from your pain" was the way she said it.

My youngest brother, Tomás, who cried about the violence inflected on us when he and I were finally able to talk about our childhood, apologized for not having protected us, his sisters. "You were only six," I reminded him. I didn't ask him what he saw or what memories he had about the abuses, but my suspicion has always been that all my siblings had witnessed random acts of incest. The conversation I attempted with my other two brothers was superficial and uncomfortable. They, like Amá, did not want to resurrect the past—too painful to remember.

As I had already broached the subject with Amá, I did not hesitate to speak with her, although when I called her I exercised care, asking her forgiveness and apologizing for stirring the memories that she still wanted to keep silent. But I had no choice. I had to confirm parts of stories where she was central. I wanted to ensure that my recollections were consonant with the rest of my family's. Though questioning the wisdom of my need to know, Amá still talked to me, told me what she remembered. I could hear the pain in her voice, yet no matter how difficult it might have been for her, she answered every question.

When the book came out and Mague finally read it, we talked for about two hours. It was then that I learned that she called our father *el cucuy*—the boogey man. She liked the book. The only reservation she had was about the pig story; she didn't want anybody laughing at her. Still, she said she loved the stories, and she apologized for not having protected us, a charge she felt was her responsibility. She added that she had no idea how hurt I had been by our father's depravity; she thought she had protected us by submitting to his demands.

Sisters, brothers, nieces, and nephews have read the book. Like me, they feel it has given them insight about the skeletons that my nephew unearthed when he found out about his conception. No one has complained, and, with the exception of how we came about my nephew's name, those who lived our life story agree I have presented an accurate portrayal of our experiences.

Why did I write the book? It was an extension of my coming to terms with the violence and my experiences in the family, just as my community organizing and social work were means of intervention and ways of preventing the abuse of the most vulnerable, as well as a desire to prevent others from going through the horrors of my family's experiences. The social work profession gave me a point of entry for helping others, providing me a place for growth and education, which deepened my knowledge about violence. Counseling and therapy helped me to further understand my own experience and to continue the healing. It was social work that brought me deeper insight about my family dynamics and how these affected me as an individual. It was Amá's ability to reclaim her life that taught us to love ourselves; it was her recognition of Juan's betrayal and her support of us that restored our self-worth. Our healing began when she took back her self-respect and integrity as our mother by refusing to believe him.

Las hijas de Juan has given me a different level of understanding. Taking me beyond self-blame, I have placed the onus of our hurt where it belongs—on our father. Acknowledging the power of writing, I see the book as a venue by which those individuals who have been victimized by incest may give voice to their experiences. On a personal level, I am still awed by the responses of those who have read it, and I feel inspired to expand the discourse of incest beyond the shame, so that we may prevent the violent destruction of women and girls who confront these abuses. I feel challenged to write the second and third books because they take the story beyond my young adulthood. The lessons I learned from the process are roadmaps for understanding the violence familiar to those of us who are physically, spiritually, psychologically, and sexually violated. What the mind buries, the body remembers in ways that we have yet to understand—self-contempt, illness, and internalized hate are but some of the manifestations.

By healing old wounds, although it has taken me more than half a lifetime, I have finally learned to embrace and love myself. Even so, I have not traveled alone. On this journey and among my loved ones—friends, my social family, and each other—there have been plenty of *madrinas* and *comadres* who have facilitated the healing. But it hasn't been easy. Some family members on Juan's side believe his lies when he claimed that my sisters and I "wanted to be libertines," or that "they pranced in front of me and tempted me." Their ignorance is unforgivable—how can girl children seduce a grown man? My immediate family has made no effort to maintain ties with those relatives.

Then there are those who still assume that my mother was complicit in the abuse, accusing her for the conditions she endured. "How could she have not known? Why didn't she see what was going on right under her nose? She must've realized something was amiss." A multiplicity of questions have been asked about Amá's blame in the process. Typically, this is an expression of the patriarchal expectations that universalize an image of a caring mother on whose skin we etch the blame for the wrongs in the family. These judgments do not even feign incredulity; they question her inability to hear, to see, or to allow herself to even suspect Juan's malice. This is what they refuse to understand: she, like the acts that were perpetrated on us, her children, was bound in the fear that framed the silence of our denial. Why couldn't they see that Amá, more than anyone, paid the price? She, who married with the expectations of creating a lifelong marriage filled with love and care, never imagined such a life. It wasn't supposed to end this way for her. No one would have guessed she'd end up alone in a broken and empty marriage that she would refuse to end because the Church had sanctioned her union.

In the end, she surprised everyone. Despite having to survive inside the tensions of those idealized expectations of the two-parent myth, when Juan was sent to prison Amá became the parent she could never be when he was part of our household. Away from Juan, we, Amá and my siblings, learned to love each other; we grew alongside her. We learned to give and accept the right touch. We relearned caring and love, as we took ownership of our bodies and minds. United, we began the process of shedding Juan's evil from our midst, coping with the consequences of his abuse—the anger, the seizures, and the broken hearts he left behind. Together, we grew and learned to deal with and overcome our past.

The publication of my book sped the healing process. Soon after I finished writing it, my younger sister Sonia visited me, bringing with her additional pieces of the puzzle—photographs of our family back in the day when we lived in Los Angeles, one of the many places we had learned to call home. It was this visit that allowed me to accept that I could make a difference in the lives of those who survived the degradation imposed by emotional, psychological, and physical violence. The book opened Sonia up to disclose what she witnessed; she could finally speak about what she saw. It was the first time Sonia and I finally talked about growing up inside our family. It was then that we purged the skeletons, bone by bone, without the fear of exposure or the silence that veiled our family's denial. Up to this time, only Felisa, Mague, and I had discussed our upbringing with bounded discretion—never treading on the incest that we all had in common. Thinking we were protecting each other from the shame, we kept the secret from the younger ones to shield and protect the family's honor.

The treasure trove of photos, the unexpected gift she brought with her, made Sonia's presence that much more valuable. The pictures she brought back from L.A. said it all. Yet, to any outsider, the degradation was not evident. They were just black-and-white images of people whose reticence in print was explained as "just looked shy," "seemed reserved," "didn't like to have her pictures taken," or "just another example of Mexican stoicism."

But the images spoke to me. My body and mind flooded with all the emotions of someone who was trapped inside her reality, and I relived the realization that I had sensed what was wrong but lacked the trust, confidence, and support to name it. The shadows and postures mirrored the invisibility to which we were relegated. They reminded me of what others and I had failed to see, could not see, or did not want to see. We carried in our bodies what we were living.

Those images filled my memory gaps. Aghast at what I saw, I finally understood Amá's gripping fear. I finally recognized that Amá barely managed. She was a ghost-walker of abuse, doing what she could to stay alive.

One Polaroid picture of Amá said it all; her injuries were etched on the lines of her posture. This was not the proud woman I had learned to appreciate. My *llorona*-like mother stumbled through life on a threadbare wire of survival. She was thinner than I remember. Her hair was disheveled, partially covering her face. The image did not reflect the Amá of my childhood. She resembled a Holocaust survivor, residing inside the torture chamber of what she had hoped would be domestic bliss.

Those were the days when denial and denigration colluded so that we could stay alive, as every one of us kept the unspoken pact of silence. When the others and I, who was the smart one and the *metiche*, who saw all, were blinded by our fear, we were muted by the violence. We overlooked what was in front of our faces to stay alive. Experiences long buried came back with those images. The photographic retrospective was but one of the many visits we had with each other after the book. We sisters finally culled recollections buried, acknowledging each other's memories. Attempting to cast out the injuries, we shed tears to release the pain that no longer served us.

Since then, I have reexamined other photographs. They document the state of our bodies and our minds. They are a testament to our survival, and they help us mourn the loss and put faces to experiences. In some pictures we were just walking shadows doing time in the purgatory that had become our lives, surviving inside the hell created by the man who never earned the right to be called father. In others, I could almost make out the call for help that never came. *El monstruo. El cucuy. El viejo.* Those were the names we used to refer to Juan, who was gripping even in his absence—we carried him in our fear.

Stories of survival were part of our legacy. Depleted but victorious, we were women warriors; that's how we saw each other. In the in-between space of our ambivalence—the tension of our betrayal and survival—we found our core; *coraje y corazón* had been the link to our survival. In the memories of our betrayal, we shed the hurt from the repeated physical, psychological, and spiritual bankruptcy that fed Juan's ability to violate our trust. We stripped him of the power he held over us. Peeling his messages of worthlessness, we began to thrive.

Family issues aside, my daily struggles continue, although not as ominous as the ones my family and I survived. Since *Las hijas de Juan* was first published, colleagues have asked in what ways the book is a contribution to sociology. I have offered that my book is a *testimonio* of my experiences in which I engage a collective retelling of our history, where members of my family have confirmed, verified, and affirmed the text I wrote. As is the case with most women who break the code of silence, speaking out has marginalized me among some of my peers. I don't think they see or understand the value in my story. Yet, the book has also opened spaces for discussion at various community venues: private Catholic high schools, universities, and other public spaces. In those spaces, I speak about the book as a testimony of a family experience narrated by me as an insider, where our emotions were central in overcoming the power and control of our father. It is a story told by a girl-child who is not yet a woman, who recognized her own value despite feeling branded by the experience and choked by the jagged recollections. I am grateful that *Las hijas* has opened space for discussion among many communities.

Still, there were those who question whether I am reproducing a culture of poverty or casting a blame-the-victim light on my family's story. Such charges have been made. "What makes you think that your account will not be misconstrued as another culture of poverty argument of the Mexicano experience? I don't think women have *to tell* in order to heal."

These words have echoed inside my mind since the first academic presentation of my book. They guide my listening, as I hear hundreds of people tell me their story, and when I read the e-mail comments or the letters sent by those who have read *Las hijas de Juan*. Invariably, they do not blame or judge my mother, my sisters, or even me. Their words target Juan, who abused his power by absconding from his responsibility of care and for destroying the lives of the girls he sired. Rather than blame, they speak with compassion and understanding.

As for me, telling the stories, I have had to get back inside the subjectivity of telling from the core of my being. This process has been a constant inward, outward, and all-around self-analysis, a reflective process that engages my thinking about social violence and incest in particular. This has been an affirmation of what I have experienced, without placing the blame on those members of my family who could not or were not able to protect my sisters and me.

Since the book, I am better able to trust my reading of certain situations and I find that I am more likely to rely on my intuition. This has been a positive outcome. Without really trying, I have become aware that I intuit incest in my environment, particularly in those who have been violated, although there have been times that I have sensed perpetrators in my midst. I have learned to see those who have experienced what I have as wounded individuals with the potential to heal, instead of as victims who dwell in their hurt.

With empathy, I listen for their story. Rather than project my experiences on those who want to speak, I await theirs. To demonstrate the self-love that leads to forgiveness—for it is the wounded that we severely judge—I try to abstain from judging those who were not able to prevent the intrusion and violation of their bodies. It's not always easy. Sometimes my anger gets the best of me, but most of the time I'm able to listen with compassion and love.

The process of healing takes place in those internalized spaces of the memory of those who experienced incest as they reclaim their story in their own way—whether in journal form, in a confessional, or in a public voicing of the past. My journey bears similarities to those of some of the people who finally speak and write about their experiences. Although our family's life is a Mexican immigrant story, the wounding-in-common we share provides the base for others to understand the process of healing. While I acknowledge experiences that bind us, I also recognize that incest engages a multilayered examination of self and other. Also, I have come to accept that the memories, when you have them, do not dissipate. The body has a way of remembering violence in all its sensory complexity.

Presently, those who write about the family, and incest in particular, have simplified what it means to live inside a sociocultural, emotional, and psychological environment, assigning the power to men while relegating women and girl children to a dependency that binds them to the father. Multiple explanations abound to examine this distortion of power and abuse of authority at the individual and societal levels, albeit not framed in a social violence analysis. These arguments of individuation, dressed in sexual fantasies that can be resolved only in a triadic resolution of the Oedipal complex, reinforce the inequalities found inside the heterosexist patriarchal family form. In these psychoanalytic mindscapes, where gender and sexual power inequities become normalized, rests the conundrum for the ultimate betrayal of incest.

The very values, beliefs, and actions about who we are as girls or women are embedded in the relationships we have to ourselves and to those who are construed as having more power than we. Silence and complicity with hierarchies of socialization through the family, church, and other institutions continue to restrict how we act as sexual and sensual beings. Structures of inequality that further complicate the ways we understand ourselves and others and the ethnic and socioeconomic circumstances of our social location complicate the ways we understand or shape our sexual lives. Ideologies serve to reproduce the structural inequalities that continue to subordinate those who lack power. There is no shame in exposing those spaces of inequality.

It is those beliefs that have compelled me to write *Las hijas de Juan*. Still, though feeling resolved about my violent life experience, I find myself emotionally entangled when reading my narrative to audiences, listening to stories, and reading confessionals about incest. The social violence that promotes unequal treatment and subordination of women and girls and the myth of the home as a safe space reside in the imaginary lives of those who promote family models that keep to their script and normatively maintain their functions to keep the family in balance.

My family's story is not about the culture of poverty, although some have made a case for it. Recognizing the agency that we had, with the stories I tell, it is about coming to awareness and our formation of consciousness as we purged the violence.

To change the sociocultural conditions that reproduce violence against women and girls, we must begin by stepping outside the denial, as we challenge our society to shed the secrecy and silence. Telling is but one strategy for healing. The context and confidence of the wounded must determine the forum. If we are to change the environment that allows denigration and abuse, we must create the receptivity to hear and believe the stories when women come to voice their experiences.

Our bodies and minds map our experiences. Recognizing that knowledge resides in what we have lived, I decided to speak those stories. Acknowledging that those memories will never go away, I remind myself that they have less power over me, especially as I willfully chart my way toward change. Those *recuerdos* of long ago keep me mindful of listening and hearing those who hide secrets when they tell. As a cartographer of recollection who mapped her own survival, I pledge to hear, to believe them when they speak. And acting on their behalf, I will continue to heal.

Ultimately, the remembering and writing process was, as Gloria Anzaldúa writes, "a bridge home to the self" from the "overlapping space between different perceptions and belief systems"* and the trauma itself. Simultaneously, *Las hijas de Juan* is about the telling of our story and the emotional confusion of a family where sexual exploitation at its worst controlled our reality, where for our own self-preservation my sisters and I became experts at reading and managing the environment we inhabited.

* Gloria E. Anzaldúa, "now let us shift . . . the path of conocimiento . . . inner work, public acts," in *This Bridge We Call Home: Radical Visions for Transformation*, ed. Gloria E. Anzaldúa and AnaLouise Keating (New York: Routledge, 2002), 541.

It is inside this in-between space, in the ambivalence of a world of survivors that I tell the stories, myths, and *cuentos* of our family. It was there that I found the words of consolation that soothed my pain. More than anything, my book is a call to action. It is a mirror where others may see themselves and thus gain the power to speak about their dehumanization, with the hope of creating change and gaining spiritual renewal.

Songs Quoted in Text

Page 3. "Mexico lindo y querido." Composed by Chucho Monge. Sung by Jorge Negrete. A singing movie star during the golden age of cinema, México's beloved *charro* died December 26, 1953.

Pages 23–25. "Amorcito Corazón." Composed by Manuel Esperón-Urdinales. Sung by Pedro Infante in his role as Pepe el Toro. This signature song was featured in a film trilogy about the lives of the rich and poor of Mexico City.

Page 26. *A la víbora de la mar* is a children's game similar to London Bridge, in which children form a bridge and let some pass, while others get trapped and have to be kicked out of the game.

Page 32. "La cama de piedra." Composed by Cuco Sánchez and José Refugio Sánchez Saldaña. Sung by Cuco Sánchez.

Page 41. "A donde iran los muertos" is a line from a *norteño* song by Lalo González, "Piporro."

Page 45. "Tu y las nubes." Composed and sung by José Alfredo Jimenez.

Page 46. "Qué seas feliz." Composed by Consuelo Velázquez, one of the greatest composers of love songs during the *epoca de ora* of the Mexican cinema. Sung by María Victoria and Los Tres Ases, among others, it is a song of unrequited love.

Page 79. "Mexicanos, al grito de guerra." These lines are from the Mexican national anthem, with lyrics by Francisco González Bocanegra and music by Jaíme Nunó.

Page 81. "Buscando abrigo y no lo encontraran" is a line from "Las Golondrinas," composed by Ricardo Palmerin.

Page 83. "El Rey." Composed and sung by José Alfredo Jimenez, a composer of *corridos* and other *mariachi* songs. His music still fills the airwaves, as he has a large following. This song is often heard in the bars and ice houses of México and the United States.

Page 91. "Margarita." Composed by R. Melon-R Sánchez. Recorded by Little Joe y La Familia as well as other *norteño* groups. The song is still a favorite of my sisters.

Page 92. "La mujer de Don Simón." A ditty I learned from my great-aunts. I was unable to find a history for the song.

Page 112. "No soy monedita de oro." Composed by Cuco Sánchez and José Refugio Sánchez Saldaña. Sung by Cuco Sánchez.

Page 112. "Reloj." Composed by Roberto Cantoral. This ballad was first played in the early 1950s.

Page 112. "Payaso." Composed by Fernando Z. Maldonado. Sung by Javier Solis. This rendition came out in the early 1960s.

Page 113. "Mal hombre" is Lydia Mendoza's signature song. From South Texas, she was the first Mexican American woman of her time to record and perform Mexican music in the United States.

Page 139. "Que lejos estoy del suelo donde he nacido" comes from "Canción Mixteca," a song of farewell and longing for the land that was left behind. Composed by J. López Alvarez, it is now the property of José J. López Monroy.

Page 155. "The Town I Live In." Sung by Willie G. and The Midnighters. It was first released in the mid-1960s.

Page 159. "She kept her head in a jar by the door." From "Eleanor Rigby." This Beatles song, composed by Lennon and McCartney, was first released in 1966.

Page 166. "You sure are looking good! You're everythin' that a big bad wolf could want." From "Little Red Riding Hood." Sung by Sam the Sham and the Pharos. It was released in 1966.

Glossary

Acualaistas Roasted wild casaba seeds

Agringó Anglicized

Alambrista Border fence jumper; literally, "acrobat"

Alcahueta One who colludes

Aleluyas Holy rollers

Andanzas Wanderings

Andariega Wanderer

Arrimados Freeloaders

Baritas Twigs

Barullo Noise

Bigotona Woman with a mustache

Birria Meat from beef head

Bocona Mouthy

Bolitas Dots or little balls

Bombilla Round glass cover for kerosene lamps

Bracero A temporary worker employed under contract through an agreement between the United States and México

Bulto Eerie shadow, apparition

Cabrón An adolescent goat; used as an insult

Cachetonas Big cheeks

Cada venida de Obispo A rare occurrence; literally, "Each visit by the bishop"

Caló Language or code of *pachucos*

Cebollitas verdes Scallions

Cemitas Sesame bread

Chamuco The charred one, i.e., the Devil

Charreadas Mexican rodeos

Charro Horseman

Chata Round face

Chichi Breast

Chillonas Crybabies

Chilpayata Child

China Curly top or Chinese girl

Chinches Bedbugs

Chingada Fucked

Chingón Big and bad, or a fucker

Chipote Bulge

Chiquilladas Kids' pranks

Chirriona Tomboy

Chisme Gossip

Chonis Undies

Clica Gang or group

Cochina Dirty pig

Cochinadas Filthy things

Cola Ass

Comadre Co-mother, godmother

Compa A form of *compadre*, used for godfather or friend

Cristero Follower of the Catholic Church who rebelled against the Mexican government during the Cristero War

Cueritos en chile verde Pork rinds in chile verde

Cuernudo Horned one

De pilón Practice of giving just a little extra to entice someone back; appreciation and enticement

Desobligado Good-for-nothing

De tal palo tal astilla Like father like son; literally, "As the wood is, so is the splinter"

Disparates Stupidities

Escuincles Brats

Espantos Ghosts

Fregados Poor or badly off

Fregazos Smackings or blows with fists

Garra Rag

Garritas al aire Airing dirty laundry, i.e., exposing secrets

Godorniz Quail

Grosero Rude one

Güeras/os Whites

Guisos Fried side dishes

Harina la Piña Brand name of flour to make tortillas

Hechando vigas Cussing

Hollo Mara Mara Hole—nickname for region of Los Angeles

Huapango Type of song associated with the Postosí region of México

Huele de noche A kind of ivy plant; literally, "smells-at-night"

Inglés mocho Broken English

Ínqueser To kneel

Jetas Rude word for lips or vaginal lips

Jorobado Hump- or hunch-backed

Limones Lemons; name given to INS vehicles for their green color

Lonja Fat tire or roll

Mandado Grocery

Mañanitas Early morning serenade to celebrate a birthday

Mañoso Deviant, one who has bad habits, or one who is a pervert

Mensas Dummies

Métanse, metidas Get inside, kept inside

Metiche One who meddles

Miona Pisser

Mojadas Wetbacks

Mojones Chunks

Monda Beating; literally, "skinning"

Mordida Bribe

Mujeriego Womanizer

Muladar Dump

Nalga Ass

Nata Cream that rises to the top of boiled milk

Norteña Music identified with northern México; usually includes an accordion

Orejones Big ears

Pa' acabarla de fregar To top it off

Pachuco/Pachuca Gang-identified Chicano

Panocha Brown sugar; vagina

Parbulito Kindergarten

Pata rajada Indian; literally, "cracked foot"

Pedos Farts or drunkards

Pelado Rabble or rude person

Pendejo Stupider than stupid

Pepitas Roasted pumpkin seeds

Pesados Ruthless

Pinacate Beetle

Pinche Fucking

Pinguillas Brats

Pito Flute; penis

Plaso Waiting period between engagement and wedding

Pláticas Heart-to-heart talks

Pleitos de familia Family feuds

Pochas Individuals of Mexican descent who speak broken Spanish

Podrido Putrid

Pretendientes Suitors

Pujidos Moans

Quelites Wild greens cooked with cactus as a side dish

Quinceañeras Fifteenth birthday celebrations

Ranchera Folk music

Rebozo Mexican shawl

Redadas INS raids

Resongona Sassy mouth

Riatas Lassos or lariats

Robachicos Child stealers

Romantica Ballads

Rucas Old ladies

Santa señora del mes Holy woman of the month, i.e., menstrual cycle

Segunda Secondhand store

Soflamaron Embellished

Solitos Ability of baby to stand by itself

Sonso Dummy

Sopa de fideo Vermicelli soup

Suato Stupid

Taco de ojo Eyeful

Tatemadas Cooking in an open-air pit with embers of mesquite

Temachaca A type of tree; the new growth is pinched off and cooked in a soup

Tina Tin bucket

Tisnada Burnt one

Trompuda Big-lipped

Tsenzontles Larks

Tunas Prickly pears

Vaquera Cowgirl

Vatos Guys

Verdolagas A wild succulent plant cooked as a side dish

Viejo volado Dirty old man

Vireinato de Zacatecas North central region of New Spain carved out by the Spanish king

Wisas Girls or girlfriends

Yagas Scars

Yunaitis United States

Zancudos Mosquitoes

Zonso Dummy; from *zoncear*, to goof around

Josie Méndez-Negrete is an associate professor of
Mexican American Studies at the University of Texas,
San Antonio.

Library of Congress Cataloging-in-Publication Data
Méndez-Negrete, Josie.
Las hijas de Juan : daughters betrayed / Josie Méndez-
Negrete.—Rev. ed.
p. cm. — (Latin America otherwise)
ISBN-13: 978-0-8223-3880-2 (cloth : alk. paper)
ISBN-10: 0-8223-3880-7 (cloth : alk. paper)
ISBN-13: 978-0-8223-3896-3 (pbk. : alk. paper)
ISBN-10: 0-8223-3896-3 (pbk. : alk. paper)
1. Méndez-Negrete, Josie—Childhood and youth.
2. Mexican American women—Biography. 3. Mexican
Americans—Biography. 4. Migrant agricultural
laborers—United States—Biography. 5. Incest
victims—United States—Biography. 6. Child sexual
abuse—Case studies. 7. Mexican American families.
8. Mexican American women—Social conditions.
9. Women's rights—Case studies. 10. Family
violence—Case studies. I. Title. II. Series.
E184.M5M465 2006
305.48'86872073092—dc22   2006008058

Las hijas de Juan

A book in the series

Latin America Otherwise:

Languages, Empires, Nations

Series editors:

Walter D. Mignolo, *Duke University*

Irene Silverblatt, *Duke University*

Sonia Saldívar-Hull, *University of California, Los Angeles*